TO THE EDGES
OF THE WORLD

KATHY McCULLOUGH

TO THE EDGES
OF THE WORLD

KMC Publishing
Somewhere in Oregon

CONTENTS

INTRODUCTION

Piloting a Boeing 747 around the world, we joked about flying from layover to layover. Two and three days off in foreign countries seemed more like a vacation than a job. The other crewmembers laughed as I "hit the ground running," and often came sightseeing with me.

My love of traveling started when I was small. Each summer my parents sent my brother and me to live with our grandparents. I traveled by planes, trains, and automobiles from Delaware to Indiana and back for as long as I can remember. The first time I flew on an airplane, the flight attendant let me pass out Chicklets gum to the rest of the passengers. Another time we hit severe turbulence while eating, and I used my fingers like window wipers to clean the gravy off my glasses. Flying was part of my world early on, and it seemed like an adventure.

As you sit in your living room reading a travel book, it should transport you.

From Europe to Asia, Alaska to Antarctica,
come fly with me!

CHUM

This smiling, handsome deckhand saved my life one night. I was on a ferry en route from Batam, Indonesia to Singapore. 9/11 had just happened and we, as Americans, were suddenly the enemy. People in Southeast Asia seemed happy that our country had been attacked. Street markets had cell phone covers and T-shirts for sale with 'Bin Laden Hero' written on them, along with his picture. The open friendliness and smiles that were once plentiful in Singapore were rarer and the dislike on their faces unnerved me.

My employer, Northwest Airlines, had been proactive seven years before when the Bojinka Plot was exposed. They had removed the word "Orient" from our name and stripped the painted stars and stripes of our flag from our planes. They credited these actions with our airline not being one of the targeted ones, as United Airlines with American Airlines with their names and red, white, and blue paint schemes were. Our company began matching up luggage with passengers years before 9/11, removing those without their 'owners' onboard. Our cleaners were crawling under seats checking for bombs, while mechanics checked ceiling compartments and other areas. We were told to remove any stickers or symbols on our flight bags that could identify us as Americans. I stopped wearing my U.S. flag pin on my uniform jacket. When asked where I was from, I told people "Canada."

Despite my precautions, I had accidentally boarded the workingman's ferry heading back to Singapore after visiting friends. Here I was, the only female and the only American aboard an Indonesian ferry as dusk fell. *So much for being careful in a Muslim country.* The looks I was getting from my fellow passengers implied they would rather slit my throat than be on a ferry with me. They weren't even trying to hide their hatred.

I was so scared. The water was dark, and there were no lights reflecting off the surface. I feared I might be chopped up and used as chum to feed the fish in the South China Sea. No one would know what happened to me if I disappeared. At least it would be a short trip, one way or another.

The deckhand was the only person who was friendly to me. We talked nonstop, and I followed him everywhere. I watched him coil the ropes and reset the anchor. He took down the Indonesian flag and put up Singapore's. From deck to deck, I was his shadow, and I don't think he knew why. When the ferry pulled into the Singapore terminal, I told my new friend goodbye and ran for the nearest taxi. I was alive!

I never went back to Batam after that trip. Even the tourist ferry had been uncomfortable on the way over that morning. It was sad, because I loved going there. I remember the first time I went...

BATAM, INDONESIA

Singapore is just a hop, skip, and jump from Indonesia. After seeing Singapore thirty or forty times, I decided to do something new. I had flown over Batam, the closest Indonesian island, many times on my way into Changi Airport, yet I had never visited.

I pointed out the island to the captain and copilot as we descended into Singapore on arrival the night before. Neither of them wanted to go with me. When I asked the lady at the front desk what there was to see and do, she told me Batam was boring—just beaches and jungle—unless you were a golfer. I wasn't deterred. Ferries left the Singapore harbor for Batam hourly, so it would be easy to get there. Besides, a friend at church was collecting foreign money for his grandsons and I hadn't brought him Indonesian rupiahs yet.

I woke up early and dressed, ready for the day. Leaving my room, the copilot's door opened as I walked by. "Do you want company?" Bill asked. Of course I wanted company! Exploring a foreign country alone is never my preference. We took a cab to the main ferry terminal, where we bought our tickets and began our adventure.

Pilots don't get the usual paperwork entering Singapore that tourists do. We only had a small, white piece of paper instead of a passport stamp. We were taken into a back room at the ferry terminal to be 'processed' by customs. It felt more like an interrogation. They wanted to know when we had arrived in Singapore, and when were we leaving. Why were we going to Batam and what were we were going to do there? It took so long that we missed our boat. They finally gave us temporary paperwork and we caught the next ferry.

Leaving Singapore was exciting. "K" Line containers were piled like tall buildings on the shore, waiting to be loaded by giant cranes. We stood outside on the ferry deck, watching all the activity as we pulled away from the dock. Highrises had replaced most of the mangrove swamps, yet the harbor was still being dredged to create more land for Singapore. There were tankers from all over the world looming around us—huge hulks of steel rising from the sea—as we maneuvered between them to get out of the harbor.

There is so much to see on the forty-minute trip across the Singapore Strait. Countries I've never heard of have cargo ships: Latvia, Estonia, Lithuania, Malta. Cargo decks are piled high with giant boxes and look so unstable. I wonder how many storage containers have fallen off these freighters and are submerged just below the surface. Indonesian ferries have horrible safety records, and swimming in this water would be disgusting and possibly fatal. Floating debris is everywhere, and I look for crocodile eyes, because I've heard there are saltwater crocodiles here.

I'm too excited to dwell on morbid thoughts for long. The island of Batam appeared out of the haze. The sky cleared and the boat slowed. Now I could make out the shoreline. People were fishing in small boats. There were grass huts and palm trees, exactly what I had envisioned and hoped for. This was like a trip back in time after being in modern cities like Singapore, Hong Kong, and Osaka. We pulled into Sekupang, a ferry terminal with traditional Indonesian architecture and rooflines.

Clearing customs in Batam was easy, and we walked into the terminal with our newly stamped passports. Surrounded by shouting and hawking, one cab driver was especially forceful. His English was good, so we followed him to his car. He asked us where we were going. *We didn't have a clue.* He suggested a resort, and we agreed on his more than reasonable fee for all day: ten American dollars.

We bounced along hard-packed dirt roads. Women in colorful print dresses carried full baskets on their hips or heads. Children followed behind, or played alongside the road. The 'town' of Batam was a joke, with a few two-story buildings stretching a block or so. Most of the structures seemed dilapidated and empty. The lady at our front desk was right. There wasn't much to see except an occasional glimpse of the South China Sea.

The driver asked if we would like to eat at a typical Indonesian restaurant over the water on the way to the resort. Of course we said yes! He drove us down a dusty jungle road in the middle of nowhere. The trees cleared and the dust settled as we parked in a clearing with shacks and a restaurant. The sign said Batu Besar. Getting out of the cab into the sweltering heat and humidity, we could hear monkeys chattering in the trees above us. On the walkway into the restaurant there were cages filled with small animals and birds. A porcupine rattled its quills as we passed, sounding like a loud rattlesnake. Monkeys peered through the bars at us, extending their hands for treats. Tropical birds I had never seen before hopped from perch to perch. Roosters strutted about as dogs and kids played in the yard.

Set on pilings among the mangroves, the restaurant was more like a dock with a railing and a grass roof. Glass tanks lined the entry, and we were invited to choose our entrées. I wondered: *Are the porcupine and other animals for atmosphere or dinner?*

Sitting under the thatched roof, we ordered two Bintangs, the local beer. The heat gave way under a slight breeze off the water, and the temperature was perfect. A small band appeared to serenade us, the only patrons. For three hours we gorged ourselves on spicy chili crabs and delicious Indonesian rice dishes full of prawns. We relaxed completely in our newfound world, amid the chatter of monkeys and children in the distance. I admired the shells in the water and the owner's son dove in and brought them to me!

The bill, in rupiahs, equaled thirty-two U.S. dollars. It was unbelievably cheap considering how much we ate and drank. Sadly, we said our goodbyes.

Our driver took us to a resort that was only three miles away. The foliage along the road was lush and impenetrable. We could see monkeys swinging from tree to tree. We rounded a corner and saw thatched-roofed villas overlooking a freeform pool and the South China Sea. Exactly what I had hoped for.

Walking through the resort was like being in a wonderland. The grass huts were staggered in the verdant foliage, with balconies and amazing views of the water. There was a chess set with pieces the size of small children. The pool had a swim up bar, but no patrons. Beautiful foliage and flowers lined the paths around the grounds and down to the water. Again, the place was deserted except for us. There was a temple at the end of a long pier. I wandered toward the beach and waded in and out of the waves, stooping to pick up shells. There were hundreds more on the beach… shells I had only seen in the Bailey Matthews National Shell Museum in Florida. *Heaven.*

Bill was not as enthralled as I was. Melting in the heat, he just wanted another beer. He agreed to walk out to the temple with me if I would go back to the resort pool-bar afterwards. The 'temple' turned out to be a bar overlooking the South China Sea. We never made it back to the pool.

We spent the rest of the afternoon watching life go by. Indonesian farmers burn their fields this time of year, and when we left Singapore, it was under a smoky haze. Batam had clear skies and expansive South

China Sea views. Air Malaysia jets landed at an airport nearby as we sipped our beers. There was another ferry terminal less than a mile away, we learned, and the ferries ran until nine that night. "This is incredible!" we said over and over again as we sat admiring the view. At last we took the six o'clock boat home, and watched the sun set on the water. Because of the smoke, the sun was a huge, fiery-red ball. I slept like a baby that night, full of dreams of the day.

THE NEXT MORNING, climbing out of Singapore in our 747, the captain asked how the trip to Batam had been. Bill and I looked at each other, at a loss for words. Where should we begin? "You should have gone," we finally said, in unison. The flight attendant brought up hot coffee, warm croissants, and freshly squeezed orange juice. It was a perfect end to our vacation at the end of the world.

Life can be perfect. For a brief time.

Alex on the balcony at Turi Beach
Alex with me at their house that overlooked the China Sea (Yes, it is hot!)

BACK TO BATAM

Years later, my mom and I visited my birthplace, Dover, Delaware. One of Mom's closest friends, who I called 'Aunt' Jane, learned that I flew to Singapore. She wanted me to visit her son and his family who were living on Batam. I procrastinated for a few months, hating to fill a long, restful layover meeting people I didn't know. I finally called when I had a two-day layover.

The connection was horrible. Over the crackling phone line, Lisa, Aunt Jane's daughter-in-law, told me what ferry company to use and how to get there. She said her driver, Tara, would meet me at customs.

Again, it was easy to get to the ferry terminal by cab. The customs officers in Singapore took me into the familiar back room to warn me about going to Batam alone. An unescorted female is not safe in this dangerous part of the world, they told me. I'm glad they were concerned. They were mollified when I told them a driver was meeting me and that I would be with friends who were locals. I was given the necessary documention and led back to the waiting room. I found a phone and struggled to use a calling card to tell Lisa what time and ferry I would arrive on… cell phones were a convenience of the future, and rare.

Out on the open water, my excitement began to build. The people onboard were friendly and we struck up conversations. I met coffee farmers from Sumatra who said their soil was so rich that it is like my wet coffee grounds at home. I commiserated with a pilot for Singapore Airlines as he told me about his awful schedule and his $5,000 a month apartment rent. Golfers talked about the cheap golfing on Batam, and a businessman said he was going over to inspect an American computer chip factory located there.

It was a fast trip. We docked at the terminal with its beckoning rooflines, surrounded by mango trees. Clearing customs, I was barraged by hawkers and taxi drivers. Tara stepped up and introduced himself and they backed off. As we crossed the road, I could see Lisa waving to me outside the car. She was the only blond American in the parking lot, just like she said she would be. Lisa spent her high school years in Dover, Delaware—I spent my grade school years there. I live at the east end of the Columbia Gorge in Oregon—Lisa grew up in Corbett on the west end, only two hours from me! We became friends, bonding in minutes. The kids, Alex and Brian, were adorable, and I could see why their grandmother missed them so much.

DRIVING TO LISA'S house, the dusty streets look familiar, but Lisa tells me things have changed since my last visit. The island population has grown too fast for what little infrastructure there is. Batam grew from an island population of 100,000 to over a million in just a few years. The immigrants are all hoping a corporation will hire them, but there are hundreds of thousands of people vying for only a few jobs. People live in *kelongs*—platforms built into the sea—if possible, so they can catch fish. Or they pick out a banana tree, set up a hammock, and stake out their rooster.

Prostitution is rampant, Lisa tells me. Prostitutes hang out in grocery stores, on street corners, golf courses, and hotels… literally everywhere. They are looking for wealthy foreign men, like her husband. Of course, all foreign men are wealthy to them. The bar waitresses practice voodoo, spiking drinks with their menstrual blood, Lisa says. I shudder involuntarily, thinking about what a sheltered life I lead.

We are waved through at a guard shack, and pull into a nice neighborhood. Lisa and Chris live in a beautiful house provided by his employer, with a company car and driver. The house has tall ceilings and white tiled floors. Their fenced yard is filled with bananas, pineapples, beautiful flowers, toys, and a wading pool. Outside the fence is an overgrown gully full of tarps and plastic sheeted tents—what we in the United States would call a homeless camp. It is such a dichotomy between their house and the people in the gully that it is hard to comprehend. Lisa makes me promise not to tell Aunt Jane any of the bad parts of their life.

Four Indonesians help with driving, housework, cooking, gardening, and the kids. This full-time help costs two hundred U.S. dollars a month, total—fifty dollars each! Lisa shops for food and anything else they need over the Internet. Sometimes it arrives—sometimes it doesn't. Her mail is always opened before she gets it, and often her shipments are usually raided. She tells her parents *not* to put cash in birthday cards for the children, but they don't listen. The cards are always ripped open and empty.

One of Lisa and Chris' houses

We have a delicious lunch at the country club restaurant, and spend the afternoon at the swimming pool. Lisa is nursing Brian, so I play with Alex, her two-year-old, in the pool. He's so much fun, and I catch him at least a hundred times as he jumps into the water. By the end of the day, enlightened and entertained, I take the ferry home to Singapore.

Back in Singapore, the taxi queue is over an hour and a half long. After waiting in line for ten minutes, I overhear someone say they can hire a special limousine for only ten dollars more, and there is no line. It's a no-brainer and I follow them to a lineup of white, old-fashioned limousines. I sit on a long, boxy seat miles behind the driver with a huge stuffed Minnie and Mickey Mouse. People try to peer in the windows at stoplights, hoping to see someone famous inside, but the windows are tinted. I feel like a princess.

Now that I have cracked the code, subsequent trips will be much easier. I start bidding two-day Singapore layovers, so that I can spend the night on Batam. I become more and more attached to the kids, and always take them presents. We go to Turi Beach sometimes, the resort I was at years before with Bill, and for thirty American dollars, Lisa rents a day room so that Brian can take a nap. Sometimes her husband, Chris, comes with us, but usually he has to work. There are still monkeys in the trees and beautiful shells on the beach. The water of the South China Sea isn't clean enough for me to swim in, but the free form pool still has the swim up bar. It is like our private paradise. We usually have the resort to ourselves, and spend the days swimming with the kids playing Shark, or Yucky Yummy, or some other game Alex and Brian invent. I love trying Indonesian foods like *nasi goring*, and Batam is always an adventure.

Most of the expats live one resort over from Turi Beach in Nongsa. Nongsa has a marina, and it's bigger, so sometimes we go there instead. Lisa's Australian friend lives there, as well as a lady who lives on her boat and makes beautiful batik fabrics to sell to the tourists. I buy masks, dolls, and carved pieces of art to take home. Mostly I just soak up the culture and the experiences. One time we were unable to get to Nongsa. Armed guards blocked our path, and we learned Dictator Suharto was at the marina. Tara was so scared that he started shaking. Lisa and I wondered if Tara's visa was illegal, or if he knew something we didn't. He quickly turned the car around and we left.

We drive to Batu Besar instead, and I laugh when I learn it is their favorite restaurant. Tara taught Alex to fish there using a safety pin and some line. Lisa and I are surprised when Alex pulls in an angelfish. I had only seen them in fish tanks—here they are native. The angelfish is too beautiful to eat, and I'm happy they let it go. Monsoons are a common occurrence, with the warm rain coming down in sheets. The thatched roof keeps us dry and comfortable, the food is still delicious, and I wonder if Bill ever came back to Batu Besar.

SOME DAYS WE went sightseeing, and Tara drove us through the settlements along the coast. The Indonesian government was in the process of moving the people into government housing. No one wanted to move from their open-air huts into sweltering concrete buildings. The concrete housing was poorly maintained, and nothing in it worked for long, so the places fell apart within months.

Maintenance and plumbing problems were Lisa and Chris' biggest headaches, too. The quality of products on Batam was horrible. The paint was so watered down that it was always peeling, and the pipes in their homes were already rusty and leaking. I visited them in three or four different houses over the years. The houses were beautiful and had wonderful views of the South China Sea, but there were always problems, especially with the plumbing in the bathrooms and kitchens.

One day, upstairs in the boys' bedroom of their new house, I saw a hairy spider, with a body the size of my fist, outside the window. Lisa said they were everywhere, and that they had to spray three times a day to control them inside the house. I learned that I could no longer give blood back home because Batam was listed as a malarial region. I never got malaria, and neither did Lisa or the kids. Brian, unfortunately, developed seizures a few years later, which he still contends with as an adult now.

Sometimes Lisa and Chris brought the kids to Singapore to see me. We always had fun, and I couldn't imagine layovers without them. One St. Patrick's Day was the best, and we hung out at Sweet Molly Malone's where children were allowed inside the bar and given bright green balloons.

Lisa went to the only Christian church on Batan. The church was burned one Sunday after 9/11. Things seemed to fall apart after that, and I always feared for their safety. Lisa and Chris had a daughter by then, and another child on the way. Even though they lived in protected neighborhoods with a guard shacks, the guards were easily bought off. One night, two men were murdered in the street in front of their house. I was glad when they moved to Singapore, even though I missed visiting them in Batam. And I never told Aunt Jane details about their life on the island.

Some things are better left unsaid.

A Batam beach shack

THE BEST TOUR GUIDES

Cab drivers make the best tour guides. I love sitting up front with them because they seem to warm up and communicate more face-to-face. Talking to them is one of the best ways to learn about the world and how differently people think.

I always took cabs to the zoo in Singapore because of the heat and the distance. Getting into the cab, the driver's first question was always, "First time here?" They were shocked when I said no, twentieth or thirtieth! Their second question was usually, "Are you from Australia?" When things heated up after 9/11, I always answered yes, and asked how they knew. They said I was too well dressed to be an American! (I dressed in longer, more modest, shorts and I never wore jeans or tee shirts.)

My first question to the Singapore drivers was always, "How do you like living here?" Their answers were never hesitant—they either loved it or hated it. The ones who loved it seemed genuinely happy in Singapore. The ones who hated it were angry with the government for their strict control of prices, lifestyle, rules, and everything else.

Singapore is not-so-jokingly known as a 'Fine City.' You could be fined for not flushing the toilet in public places, even though most of them are electric now. The 'no chewing gum' rule was imposed in 1992 to decrease vandalism of public property. Gum was all over the sidewalk, benches, and statues. Importers are the intended breakers-of-the-law, not chewers, but I was still careful not to chew gum there. Jaywalking and littering incur fines from $300 to $1000, even for first offenses. There are rules against smoking in cabs, and huge penalties for importing drugs. Graffiti is punishable by caning, and none of this is secret. Signs are posted everywhere, starting in the airport jet bridge as you step off the airplane into their country. All these controls make Singapore a clean and safe city.

Yusof took me all over in his cab, from the richest to the poorest parts of Singapore.

My hotel on Clark Quay

One young cab driver, Yusof, took me everywhere—from the richest mansions and embassies to public housing and the poorest slums. I wanted to see the *real* Singapore, not just Sentosa Island and other tourist attractions. I wanted to see the mosques, the temples, and how the people lived. He was so excited about showing me his city that he turned his meter off! When it was time for morning prayers, he showed me his mosque. I couldn't go in dressed in shorts, so I waited outside. After driving me everywhere for more than two hours, Yusof wouldn't take any money. He wouldn't even let me tip him. He gave me his address, and I sent him copies of the pictures. I hope he got them, because I have never forgotten his kindness.

As a tourist, I like feeling safe. The cab drivers and a bouncer told me about an underground Singapore—a well-hidden Singapore—with drugs, prostitution, and gangs. They assured me I could still walk around at three in the morning and be safe. Tourists were never targeted, they said, because we are Singapore's bread and butter. There are huge repercussions for messing with tourists. I still never stayed out late alone.

Yes, Uber, Lyft, and limo drivers are great, too. I love talking to people. My girlfriends laughed at me in Washington D.C. because I made friends with every driver we had. But I learned about the Trump Hotel opening (September 2016), what the new African American museum represents (three-tiered crowns used in Yoruban art from West Africa), along with recommendations for restaurants and the best views of the Potomac (lots of great ones). An Uber driver in Gainesville, Florida turned out to be a horse trainer in Ocala who had just moved from New Jersey. What a story he had to tell!

Our cab driver in Auckland, New Zealand was a civil engineer. He and his family left Egypt because they were Christians living in a Muslim country, and he feared for his wife and daughter's safety. Rapes of Christian women were prevalent in Egypt, he said, and were rarely reported or prosecuted. Men hide under burkas, even in places that are for women only, and no one can tell who is under a burka. He couldn't find employment in his degree field when he emigrated because New Zealanders get first choice of jobs in their country. He told us he didn't mind being a cab driver. His family was safe living in New Zealand, and that was what mattered.

After listening and questioning the engineer/driver for an hour in the stalled traffic, my husband and I boarded our cruise ship with a new respect for what some people go through in this world. We wondered if our cab driver's daughter would ever understand what a sacrifice her father had made for her safety and future.

Love can never be overrated.

AN ISLAND FOR A PRINCESS

Canada is the country that firmly cemented my love of travel. Two of my most memorable trips have been to Ontario and British Columbia with men named Jack.

THE FIRST MAN was Jack Horner, a friend of my father's. Jack invited us to stay on his island in northern Ontario the summer of 1969.

Who owned an island? An entire island! My brother Jim and I were beyond excited. As soon as school let out in Florida, our family packed the car and headed north. We stopped in Dover and Boston to visit family. I love my cousins, but I could hardly wait to continue the trip.

Our first night in Canada was at a hotel in Montreal, where I found myself practicing my French as a translator for another guest who was checking in. We really were in another country! A fire alarm in the middle of the night provided more excitement, surrounded by people speaking rapid French and English as we stood together in the street.

The next day, we drove to Sudbury—a city four hundred miles west known for its nickel mines. My memories of Sudbury are of black rocks and another fire alarm in the middle of the night. We parked our car at the train station and bought tickets to Biscotasing, a tiny town at the end of the line.

My three-year-old brother, Kenny, showed his Matchbox car collection to a group of old men waiting for the train. Jim and I were trying to look calm and worldly, having been on a train before to visit our grandparents. But this was our first trip out of the United States. It was all we could do not to jump up and down.

Dad was on crutches, and Mom had Kenny by the hand. When the train pulled in, Jim and I handed all the bags up to the conductor before we boarded. We were off!

Not for long. The train came to a lurching stop, startling everyone on board. Passengers started looking out the windows, and finally the engineer explained that there were two moose on the tracks ahead. People started wandering off the train to look, so Jim and I followed. The moose were munching grass, and casually looked up as the engineer made loud noises and waved his arms. Everyone laughed as the moose continued to chew without looking up. Eventually they wandered off on their own.

The train started moving again once we were all boarded, but stopped at station after station to let passengers off. It took forever to get to our stop, but we didn't mind. There was so much to look at! Our family and an Indian woman were the only passengers left on the train when the conductor called, "Last stop, Biscotasing!" Mom was carrying Kenny. Dad brought up the rear, clumping on his canes.

DAD HAD CONTRACTED polio in the Korean War while enlisted in the Navy. "My bad luck," he told me when he and mom were first married. "It took three months to get me home. I was in the infirmary in the front of the ship, with orderlies pumping an iron lung the whole time so I could breathe, as we hit the waves and pitched up and down. I never want to see the inside of another ship in my life." The Navy doctors asked him which part of the country he wanted to spend the rest of his life in, because his polio was so severe that they expected him to be bedridden for the rest of his life.

Now, here he was on crutches doing whatever he pleased, fishing and hunting with the best of them. Of course, he needed help sometimes. Surfcasting was out of the question, so one of us had to cast into the ocean at home in Florida, then hand him the pole. Mom even bought a wetsuit so that she wouldn't freeze while casting in the winter. I tried the wetsuit once, but it was almost worse than none when the water seeped in to places where Mom was bigger than me.

Fishing at the beach with Dad was fun, even though he never failed to let me know he hated my methods.

One day I was casting and casting, waiting and waiting, while he had no bites. Finally, I begged to go jump waves. He agreed, if I would cast once more. I did, then waded into the ocean, far away from his line. I felt something wiggle under my feet. I bent down and carefully lifted a large flounder out of the sand, after I moved one foot and then the other. "Is this what we've been after all day, Dad?" I asked, holding up the large fish. Laughing, we put it in the cooler, and Dad made me swear not to tell Mom how we caught it.

Another time our family was out fishing for king mackerel in the Gulf of Mexico. "You catch 'em, you clean 'em," he said. I hated cleaning fish, so I kept throwing mine back. I was the only one catching fish, lying on top of the cabin roof, reading my book. That angered Dad most of all. "How can you be catching them when you're not even paying attention?" I grinned and told him you couldn't let the fish know you cared. "Okay, okay, I'll clean them," he said at last, after watching me throw yet another one back.

Now we would be catching fish for dinner every day on the island. Dad said Jack's island was fully equipped with everything we would need for fishing and living. It had a main house, a guesthouse, a boathouse, a generator house, a storage shed, and some other buildings. And we were almost there!

The conductor helped us with the rest of our provisions and gear. Jack was supposed to be meeting us, but he wasn't at the station. So, Jim and I lugged everything over to the general store, the only building in Biscotasing other than the train station and a boatyard. Jack emerged from the boatyard. The boats were stored underwater during the year, then pulled up and dried out for the summer. He had been busy putting the outboard onto one of the boats when the train arrived.

"The island is still an hour and forty-five minutes north by boat. You'll need to buy food for two weeks," Jack told Mom. "We'll come back to Biscotasing for more when we need to." Jack and Dad went to the boatyard while we went to the grocery store.

Flour, sugar, peanut butter, spices, oil, and other food went into two carts. We bought a ham for Sunday dinner and two huge bags of potatoes. It felt like we were shopping at the Naval commissary in Jacksonville as we piled the carts high with staples. Jack cleared out the cabin every winter so that nothing would attract unwanted animals. It seemed like we were buying everything except the dishes. The storekeeper helped us load the supplies into the two boats. Jim and I went in one of the boats with Jack. Mom, Dad, and Kenny followed in another.

Tall trees and blue water surrounded us. Jack let us take turns driving and said we could take the boat out anytime. There was also a canoe on the island we could use, he said, but be careful. Some of the islands had bears on them, and there were moose. Jim gave me a look that said, "Way too cool."

We scanned the shoreline, looking for animals and Indians. Jack said the man who sold the island to him had bought it for his wife, a Canadian Indian princess. The princess wanted to move to Florida, but her husband loved northern Ontario. He thought building her a nice enough house would make her want to stay. So, they made a deal. If she was still unhappy on the island after five years, they would leave.

Five years later the princess and her husband left for Florida. Jack and his dad bought the island and buildings for $5000.

We rounded a final bend and the island came into view. A little white house with blue shutters was nestled under huge pine trees. "A storybook house. How could the princess not have been happy here?" I asked. "That's just the guesthouse," Jack said, without really answering my question.

Securing the boats to the dock, Jack helped everyone out, even Dad. Then he gave us the grand tour. The main house, where we would all be staying, was faded white with peeling blue shutters. It had three bedrooms, a bathroom, a kitchen, and a giant stone fireplace in the living room. The shelves surrounding the fireplace were full of books, and I loved to read. The linoleum floors were covered with woven throw rugs. Comfortable couches and chairs filled the room, and the light streamed in through dirty windows.

The bedrooms were homey, with wrought iron headboards and beautifully quilted bedspreads. Jack's mom had decorated both houses. Jack had aired the place out, scrubbed the floors, and put on fresh bedding. "Can you handle the rest of the clean up?" he asked. We nodded, game for anything.

"We'll get the windows washed tomorrow," Mom said. "The café curtains need to be washed, too."

Jack showed us the washing machine—an old, hand-crank, wringer model. It looked like fun!

Next, he took us to the smaller house. Far away from the big house, it was nestled into a small cove. The whole upstairs was one big bedroom, and the fireplace opened onto both floors. The living room was cozier, and the kitchen was smaller. It was secluded, and I liked it even better than the big one.

The island was only a mile long and a half-mile wide. Jack said we could explore after we unloaded the boats. Jack, Jim, and I carried everything in while mom put things away. Dad watched Kenny. Then Dad, Kenny, and Jack went to the generator shed to make sure everything was working right while I finished helping mom.

At last it was time to explore! Mom was worried about us exploring the island alone, but Jack reassured her and said there was no way we could get lost. "Bears don't come around unless there's food, and moose make their presence known. We don't get many of either." He pointed us down a path in the opposite direction of the honeymoon cabin.

Dad holding a Walleye (above) and Kathy and Kenny washing clothes (below)

The "big" house on the island (above)
Jim, Kathy, and Kenny sitting on the dock (below)

Jim and I set off. We found four more buildings on the island, for a total of seven. We went into the last one. Jim said, "Hey, look, there's a phone. Who would call you out here?" Just then the phone rang, scaring us half to death.

I wasn't sure where the mouthpiece was. "Hello?" I put the bell-shaped part to my ear and listened to the tinny voice. It was our mom.

"Listen, Jack says not to eat any of the berries on the island. They're good for the birds, not people. And if you need anything, there's a phone in every building, so just call," she said.

"How? How do you call?" I asked.

"You pick up the receiver, turn the handle a few times, and then wait. If I hear it, I'll answer. If not, keep trying, or come back to the house and get me! It's probably just as fast." Jim heard every word because the receiver was more like a speaker, just cracklier. What a hoot! A phone in every shed. What a guy wouldn't do for his princess!

Walking through the underbrush, off the beaten path, a huge turkey grouse flew up in front of us. We jumped, and then laughed. It was an amazing feeling being so far from civilization.

"Phew! What's that smell?" Jim asked, holding his nose. I got a whiff of the same, awful scent. We were on the shoreline, but there wasn't anything out in the water. When we walked back in the direction of the house, the smell was fainter. But it got stronger to the west, or at least what we thought was west.

"Ugh! Here it is!" Jim said. A huge, bloated, dead moose lay in some weeds on the bank. It was the most disgusting thing I had ever seen or smelled. We backed away, holding our breath, and kept exploring until we were back at the main house.

Bursting through the door, we talked on top of each other. "What a cool island! There are paths everywhere, and birds, and all kinds of sheds. We even found a dead moose."

Jack looked up from cleaning the fireplace. "You found a dead moose? Where?" He looked worried.

"On the other end of the island, near the shore. But don't worry, we didn't touch it or anything," Jim said.

"No, it isn't that. The smell will attract bears, and once you have a bear on your island it's hard to get rid of him. Can you find it if we take the boat?" Jack asked, already moving toward the door.

"Sure. It was near one of the sheds and a big tree," I said.

"Why don't you go back there and wave us down from shore?" Jack suggested.

Jack and Jim headed for the boathouse to find some rope. I went back down the path to the other end of the island. It was eerie being all by myself. It was easy to find the moose again, and I stood by the shore, waiting.

I heard the motor before the little boat came into view. "Here! Here it is!" I said, holding my nose with one hand and waving the other. Jack headed straight to me and beached the boat. He hopped out into the shallow water with a rope.

"Whoa! That is rank. I'm glad you two went exploring. We need to be extra careful to keep big animals away, especially with your little brother around." He had gloves on and was busy tying the rope around the animal's body. Luckily the moose was close to the water because the boat could pull it off the shore. I didn't want to help push or shove it through the brush.

I jumped into the boat as Jack tied the rope to the stern. He pushed the boat away from the shore, started the motor, and eased the boat out into the lake. The rope went taut, and then the moose started to move. If it had rotted anymore Jack's plan might not have worked. As it was, the whole animal came away from the bank intact. Ycch. There wasn't any fur left on the carcass. It was pink and purplish and white and blue—the ugliest bloated balloon I had ever seen. The stench was still strong, even in the boat. We all had our shirts up over our noses, trying not to breathe. Once the boat got going, it was better. But it still smelled.

"Where are we going?" Jim asked.

"At least two islands away. There's a guy who lives on the next lake, but we're the only ones on this one."

Jack's eyes were watering and I realized he was trying not to gag. It was really gross. "So, do you know the guy on the next lake?"

"Sure do. He runs a hunting camp. You're not supposed to hunt game from the air, but that doesn't stop old Krebs. He just gets in his floatplane, spots the game, then lands. Not very sporting and very illegal, but out here, no one knows or cares."

I didn't think I liked Krebs very much but decided to reserve judgment. "Does he visit often?"

"Nope, not really. But he'll stop by tomorrow."

"How do you know?"

"Because he always comes if there's bait. If you're out sunbathing on the dock tomorrow, like you said you'll be, he'll see you. And he'll land." Jack smiled at Jim, as if to say, we know how guys are.

I wasn't sure how I felt about being bait. We kept our eyes peeled for a sandy spot to drag the moose onto. At last we found a good spot. It took all three of us tugging and pulling, but finally the moose was up on dry land.

Jack untied the rope from the boat and threw it on top of the moose. "Never get the smell out of it anyway."

On the way back to our island, Jack stopped at a rock in the middle of the lake. He killed the motor and kicked off his loafers. "Jump in!" he yelled as he dove overboard in his shirt and shorts.

We didn't have our swimsuits, but we were hot and smelly, so we dove in too. The water was freezing! We swam around, trying to wash off the moose smell. Teeth chattering, I dragged myself out onto the rock. It was hot and flat. Lying down, staring at the clouds, everything seemed surreal. The clouds were zooming by overhead. I didn't realize I had fallen asleep until it started raining.

Jack and Jim were dripping water on me. I jumped up and pushed Jim into the water. Jack was too big to push, but he jumped in anyway. So did I. It was still cold, but it felt good. Invigorating! No, freezing was the right word, but we didn't care. We swam for another fifteen minutes before Jack announced it was time to go get dinner.

"What's for dinner?" Jim asked.

"Well, you have a choice. Walleye or Northern Pike." Jack had the little outboard purring. He drove away from the rock, maybe three hundred feet, and stopped. He handed each of us a pole, and pulled a jar of big fat worms from his tackle box.

"When did you get these?" I asked.

"Dug 'em up while you were on your walk. The garden is well stocked. Speaking of which, it's your job to weed the garden this summer and catch dinner, okay?"

We nodded, grinning. Why not? Jack speared a worm several times, then cast into the water. Jim and I did the same.

I had a bite on my line within seconds. I set the hook, and then started reeling it in. A whopping big fish! Not as big as the barracuda we caught in the Florida Keys, but big enough for dinner. Jim had a bite, too, but his fish was fatter, with a yellowish belly.

Jack said that I had caught a Northern, and Jim's was a Walleye. "Northerns have more bones. But the meat's good. You can try them both and see what you think," Jack told us as he put them both on a leader and hung them over the side.

"Up here you can't go wrong. The fish just bite!" Jack said. We caught three more before Jack started the motor and headed for the island.

"WALLEYE OR NORTHERN Pike, which is your favorite?" Jack asked us at dinner.

"Walleye, for sure," I declared, with my mouth full. They both tasted great. Jack and Dad had cleaned and filleted them. Mom had floured, seasoned, and fried them up in an old cast iron skillet. Jim and I had peeled and wedged the potatoes. There was a certain satisfaction catching and preparing our own dinner. It was like being a pioneer.

I had three helpings. *Of fish.* Usually one was plenty, but not tonight. Maybe it was the excitement of the day and the newness of everything. Or maybe it was because the fish were so fresh, right from the lake to the pan. Whatever, I was starving!

"This is the best dinner ever," Jim said. He pulled bones out of his mouth, stacking them on the side of his plate, as he kept chewing.

"So, tomorrow, who wants to help me in the garden?" Mom asked

Jim and I both volunteered, as if we had a choice. There would be plenty of time for fishing, swimming, and exploring. The garden wasn't that big and, working together, it might take a few hours. Besides, Mom would be doing most of the housework, cooking, and cleaning, even though we would help. I just hoped she could relax and have fun, too.

JACK HAD PLANTED the garden a few weeks earlier. Already the vegetables were growing fast. Canadian summers were short, like Alaskan ones, he said. All growing things took advantage of the longer days and the warmth of the sun. Winters were so harsh and cold here that the animals had to bulk up fast to survive.

"I've got some insect repellent you're going to need," Jack informed us. "I buy it from an old trapper. He gets it from the local Indians who claim it's a secret potion passed down from generation to generation. They make it from herbs and roots, and it works, especially against black flies. The black flies come in swarms, but they won't touch you with this on."

We nodded, and slathered ourselves. It wasn't long before we realized why the repellent was so important. As we worked up a sweat, the flies appeared. But when we smeared on more of the Secret Indian Potion, the flies disappeared!

Jack had planted lettuce, corn, squash, beans, carrots, peas, and tomatoes. Potatoes were cheap, and we needed them right away, so that's why we bought them. We pulled weeds and plucked grubs. Done at last, we ran to the lake and jumped into the crystal clear water off the dock.

The canoe was upside down under the front porch, and we decided to take it out. Jack helped us get it, then found us paddles and life jackets in the boathouse.

We were allowed to go anywhere we wanted, Jack said, as long as we didn't portage out of the lake. I had never heard of portaging—picking the canoe up and carrying it over land to another body of water—and I hadn't thought of doing it. This lake was huge, so why would we go to another one?

Mom had lit up like a Christmas tree when Jack said there was a canoe. She said she would come later, when Kenny was taking his nap. Mom had been a lifeguard, teaching swimming and canoeing at camp when she was a teenager. She was the reason we even knew how to paddle.

In Florida, we had rented canoes at some of the springs and paddled around looking for manatees. Sometimes we dragged Dad's duck boat down to the pond behind our house. When we had friends over at home, we paired off to have water lily fights. One team would start out in the boat, while the other team stood on the shore. We would start pitching huge, muddy-rooted lilies at each other until we all looked like creatures from the black lagoon. Then we switched and the other team jumped into the boat. We had never capsized or been bitten by an alligator or a moccasin, even though there were plenty of them around. Maybe the noise and splashing scared them off, or maybe we had more close calls than we knew.

We set out on the Canadian lake. Birds called all around us, but there were no human sounds. "This is like being an Indian," I whispered to Jim, not wanting to break the silence as we glided through the water. This was so different. We felt truly alone.

Jack had sent us off with fishing poles and worms from the garden. Hours later, when we got tired of paddling, we fished. Just like before, we had enough fish within minutes and headed back to the island.

Beaching the canoe by the dock, Mom and Kenny came out to greet us. Kenny wanted to swim, so we took him into the lake. Jack said never let your feet stay still, or the leeches would latch on. So, we hopped around and jumped and played for a good half hour. I forgot about the fish. When I grabbed the stringer off the canoe to hand to Jack, the fish were covered in leeches. I was glad Jack had warned us not to stand still or our legs would look like this. He told us we could go catch new ones.

Just then there was a droning in the sky, the first foreign noise I had heard since we arrived.

"Kathy, do me a favor and go lie down on the dock," Jack said.

I took my towel and laid it out. It felt good to lie in the hot sun. I had goose bumps everywhere. A red and white floatplane flew over, and I put my hand over my eyes to shade the sun. That must be Krebs.

The plane made a hard left turn, coming in for a closer look, then landed on the lake and taxied up to the dock. Excited, I sat up. Jack helped tie off the plane, greeting Krebs.

Krebs took one look at me as he stepped onto the dock and said, "Damn. Jail bait."

Jack laughed.

Krebs was on his way to town to pick up two hunters and supplies but said he would stop back in a few days. We watched him taxi out and take off.

After he left, Jim and I went back out to catch more dinner. Again, the fish was delicious. This time the potatoes were mashed. Potatoes fixed different ways were the only variety, but having fish every night didn't keep us from eating like we were starving. Dad and Jack even ate fish for breakfast and cold fish sandwiches for lunch.

The huge fireplace was great for roasting marshmallows after dinner. We put puzzles together, played games, or read at night. I scoured the bookcase and found a book by Sinclair Lewis, an author I had heard of. The book, *Kingsblood Royal*, was about a man who was very rich and very prejudiced. He had a blond haired, blue-eyed daughter and he considered himself to be in a very different class from their black maid and the man who parked cars at the country club... until he was reminded that his grandmother, who died when he was young, was dark skinned.

I read until the fire burned low and turned into embers. Everyone else had gone to bed hours before. Closing the book, I stepped out the front door into the night. The sky was filled with more stars than I had ever seen, and the waves lapped at the dock. There were some birds flying in the night sky. I felt a thrill run through me, like a shiver. This was all so new, so unbelievable... it was like being in another world. Hugging myself against the night chill, I prayed, "Please, God, let this summer last forever!"

Mornings were cold, as were the nights, but the sun warmed everything up fast. One week we painted the house. Mom found some paint in the shed, and Jack said he had been meaning to get to it, but hadn't. Mom said we wouldn't mind at all, and we didn't. The house needed the paint to protect it against the harsh winters, and it would look so good afterwards. But there was one thing I hadn't counted on.

Jim and I were painting the white siding. Mom was doing the blue shutters. When she moved the first one to paint behind it, black things flew out and she shrieked, "Bats!" Jack said they were fruit bats, and not to worry. We weren't really worried, just surprised. Once they had all flown off it was okay.

Every time Mom started a new shutter she prepared herself for the inevitable... a face full of flutter. She got good at flipping and running, while we laughed.

I had never seen bats before, except in vampire movies or in zoos. They were small, and you could hear their high-pitched squeaks. I had seen bats, not birds, when I stepped outside at night.

The only bad thing about the Canadian wilds so far was that there were bugs everywhere. The repellent really worked, but we had to keep applying it after sweating or swimming, which meant we were always putting it on. We only painted in the mornings because afternoons were too hot. One afternoon Jim and I decided to go on a picnic. Jim wanted to eat our peanut butter sandwiches on the rock island Jack had showed us, where there would be fewer bugs. Jack told us we could take one of the outboards.

I was driving the boat. The water was so clear that we could see the bottom where it wasn't too deep. The fish kept jumping, birds were everywhere eating bugs, and the day was perfect. Blue skies reflected in the still water, and I saw a moose munching underbrush on one of the islands. There was a clunk and the engine stopped. Just stopped.

It was probably the cotter pin, we decided, but there weren't any in the tackle box. And there wasn't anything else in the boat we could use to improvise. So we drifted. And relaxed. And ate our lunch. It wasn't as if we were in any danger. Eventually Jack would realize something was wrong and he would come looking for us. Besides, the little boat was drifting towards land.

After two hours of drifting, we were bored, so we beached the boat and decided to explore, after putting on more of the secret bug potion. There was a trail of sorts through the brush, and probably lots of animals around, hiding. But Jack seemed to think we were safe enough or he wouldn't have let us take the boat. One island looked pretty much like the next, except there were no other islands with houses.

When we stopped crashing through the brush, we heard a boat motor in the distance. Racing back to the shoreline we waved our arms and shouted until Jack and Dad saw us and motored over. "I thought we'd never find you guys. It's a big lake!" Jack said. Kenny was with them, smiling and waving, his chubby arms rubbing on his life jacket.

"The cotter pin broke. We couldn't find another one," Jim said.

"That's because I broke one two days ago and forgot to put more in. It's my fault," Jack admitted, as he put in a new cotter pin.

We followed them home, and stopped on the way to catch dinner.

"I don't know if I will ever get used to fish biting so fast," Dad said.

"Yeah, Dad, you usually just wait for me to step on one," I said.
"Quiet about that," Dad warned, laughing.

THE LAST DAY of the week was washing day. Think about it... six people working hard and a week's worth of clothes. The pile was huge. Jack showed us how to use the wringer washer, and Jim and I took turns wringing and hanging the clothes out to dry on the line. The washer washed, but then we had to squeeze the water out of the clothes piece by piece.

In between washer loads, we painted. The house painting was coming along, and the garden was weed-free, although the weeds kept coming back. Jack was doing the high ladder painting. Dad played with Kenny. Mom and I had washed the windows on the second day, and the little house just shined.

Most days passed too quickly. Swimming and exploring were always fun. Usually we took the canoe because it was more peaceful and easier to spot animals when we didn't scare them off. It was a good thing we all liked potatoes, fish, vegetables, and fresh tomatoes, because that was always dinner. Food tasted better here—it seemed there was more flavor to it, even though our diet didn't have much variety. Jack said it was because it was all so fresh and we worked up an appetite.

Nights by the fire were fun. We would play card games, tell ghost stories, or just read. Mom popped corn, and we had brownies or cookies for dessert. It wasn't exactly like being a pioneer—the house was too comfortable and our stomachs were always full. But it felt like we were pioneers, except that we went into town every other weekend. Dad bought a red and black checked coat that he said was a lumberman's jacket, and of course we bought more potatoes and peanut butter, as well as a roast for Sunday dinner.

Our time on the island was winding down and the nights were getting colder. It was almost time to go home. It made me want to cry. I knew I would never have another summer like this one. I don't know what was wrong with the Indian princess.

I could have stayed forever.

MURDER IN CANADA:
FORTY YEARS LATER

We never know when harvest will be over, so we can't make solid plans that include reservations and tickets. Going standby in the summer is not an option, because the flights are too full. Instead we plan a driving vacation when the combines are put away. We've driven the Oregon Coast one vacation, then down to San Francisco the next summer. Another year we followed the Columbia River to its source, explored British Columbia, and had great fun as a family in Victoria, British Columbia. We hadn't seen the rest of Vancouver Island, so we decided to go back. Darcie was taking summer courses at college, so it was just my son Colton, my husband Kevin, and me.

Summer was winding down as we stopped to see my aunt and uncle on the Puget Sound before heading to Aberdeen. Their place is so nice, and my aunt is such a good cook, that their house is a vacation all by itself. Next we took a ferry across to Victoria, and drove on to Nanaimo. Our balcony overlooked a jazz festival, so we ate Nanaimo bars and listened to the music until midnight. The next day we headed west to Campbell River, and watched Colt mountain bike on Mount Washington.

I wanted to see whales. Driving farther west to Port McNeill, we rented a boat with a captain who took us out to see eagles and whales. We saw hundreds of orcas, and for two hours pods came up to our boat to examine us. A mother and baby came up to look at us, and I couldn't believe how big their eyes were. I was in heaven.

We could only rent our cabin in Campbell River for three nights, so the next night we moved to Quadra Island, just across the water. We hiked and ate pizza and watched the seals from our room on the water. Could this vacation get any better?

Jack Mould and Koti

Jack's house at the mouth of the Southgate River
Bob, Jack, Jack's friend, Colt, and Kevin after they unloaded the plane

Colt was watching floatplanes take off and land. He had flown around the United States and Europe, but only in airliners. He was probably too young to remember his helicopter ride in Hawaii. I soloed at sixteen and was a captain on a 747, yet my seventeen-year-old son had never been up in a small plane. What kind of a slacker-mom was I?

I called Corilair, a flying service in Campbell River, and arranged for an hour-long flight. It would cost $600, but for three of us that was only $200 apiece. Yes, it was expensive, but so was swimming with the dolphins—another experience extraordinaire we had paid big dollars for—and worth every dime.

Corilair called back an hour later, asking if we would be interested in a longer flight for the same price, sharing the plane with a local author on his way home. The flight would be in a larger plane, a de Havilland Beaver.

"Yes!" I said, almost cutting the lady off in midsentence.

She didn't have to say any more. I love Beavers! Beavers are big, tough-looking planes that can carry anything and everything out of the wilderness. They have only one engine, but it's a 450 horsepower radial.

We waited outside for our floatplane. It was a perfect day on Quadra Island. The water was so clear you could see fish and sometimes a seal. Colt was skipping stones on the hotel dock when the Beaver circled to land right in front of us. I could tell he was impressed, especially when it spun around and taxied up to the pier.

The pilot cut the motor and stepped out onto the float. His name was Bob, and he helped us into the plane. The back seat was a huge bench with seat belts. The cargo compartment behind the bench was packed full with an outboard motor and some plastic tubs. *How much can a Beaver hold?*

The man in the front seat turned and smiled. "Name's Jack Mould." His hair stuck out everywhere, even from his ears. He looked like one of those mountain men you hear about who come back to civilization after years of not seeing anyone. Jack must have read the look on my face, because he laughed and said he didn't usually look so grizzly. The Discovery Channel was doing a special on him and he was growing out his hair and beard because they wanted him to look like an authentic prospector.

Jack wasn't bragging; just stating a fact. "I look old, but I'm only seventy-one," he said. The dog on his lap was a small, shaking ball of white fur. Jack said, "Hates the airplane. Name's Koti."

I nodded, and introduced my family. Bob handed us headsets so we could hear him on the intercom. He said Colt could ride up front on the way home. Colt asked him how the plane would even get off the ground with so much stuff. Bob said the Beaver could carry 2100 pounds. I figured the five of us weighed around eleven hundred, and the outboard engine was maybe another three hundred pounds, so we were well within limits, not counting what was in the tubs. My husband gave me an "I hope it gets off the ground!" look. I think I nodded reassuringly!

We taxied out to the middle of the Strait of Georgia. Bob pushed the throttle forward and the engine growled. No, I mean it really roared. We wouldn't be able to hear Bob talk without the headsets on. As loaded down as we were, I couldn't believe how quickly we were up in the air. Colt looked excited, and he hardly ever shows his emotions. He loves roller coasters, and he loved the Tower of Terror, after the first time. This had to be better. The land fell away behind us and I could tell my son was in awe. Colt's used to having one little window on an airliner, but they climb so fast and fly so high that you can't take in all your surroundings. We were just skimming the treetops, staying pretty low.

Bob pointed out waterfalls and the house an actress, Michelle Pfeiffer, was building. Ritchie Brothers Auctioneers owned a lodge, and so did Longs Drugs, on islands that we flew over. Bob said quite a few movie stars have houses in British Columbia, and he pointed more of them out. There was big money below us, as we flew over islands with golf courses and mansions. We looked for mountain goats and bear, and spotted a grizzly. I hoped Jack's house was a long way away, because I loved looking at everything. Canada is so huge and unpopulated that we mostly saw blue water and tall trees, just like I had in tenth grade in northern Ontario.

Jack told us he wasn't as much an author as he was a prospector. He had been searching for lost Spanish gold mines most of his life. Jack said he was sorry he didn't have a signed copy of his book, *The Curse of Gold*, to give us. He said he had finally gotten lucky, discovering two gold mines in the hills above his house, old ones that were mined by the Spaniards. The Spaniards didn't have the equipment we have today, so Jack was sure he could get more gold out of them. Plus, he owned forty kilometers to the west of his house and eight kilometers to the north. There was a glacier on his land, and as it receded diamonds were popping up.

Wow! Gold mines and a glacier! No wonder Discovery Channel was doing a special! Jack pointed out his house on the water. He said there was a sunken galleon in his the bay and he had just obtained the salvage rights to it. "Yep, the Canadian government finally approved my claim," Jack said. The divers he hired estimated the galleon's worth at well over a trillion dollars. Jack pointed out the gold mines in the rocky cliff, but I couldn't really see them. They were just dark spots on the side of the mountain.

I could see his house as we circled to land. Jack said that the house looked a lot better before it flooded, and before thieves stripped it and stole the wiring. Bob agreed, and said he had brought it in and floated it up there. Jack said he wants to build a resort at the mouth of the Southgate River, where it empties into his bay.

Bob made the landing look easy, and said he had been there lots of times. We kissed the water, and taxied up to Jack's dock. It was a stretch to call it a dock—it was just lots of old pallets joined together. The little dog jumped out, happy to be home. A young man with a beard walked up, and the guys started unloading the plane. The outboard and the plastic boxes were just the tip of the iceberg. There were six months of supplies in the floats, including case after case of whiskey. Jack said the long, cold, Canadian nights are unbearable without whiskey.

Okay, so this plane really is amazing. I'll bet we were bumping right up against the 2100 pounds of payload, and it still leapt out of the water on takeoff.

Jack showed us around. Now I could see the caves in the hillside, but the water in the bay was too murky to see the galleon. It wasn't dirty water, just glacial runoff with that weird, gray color to it. I took some pictures and we said goodbye to Jack, the dog, and his friend. Colt wanted to stay and look for diamonds. I couldn't wait to see the television special.

Colt got up in the front seat. Bob spun the Beaver around and we were off the ground in a flash without Jack and all the cargo. We circled around Jack's place one more time, waved, and headed for home.

Bob told Colt all about the instruments, and the speeds he uses for takeoff and cruise. He explained how the constant propeller with counter weights works. Colt plans to take mechanical engineering in college, and he's always fixing equipment on our ranch, so he listened and asked lots of questions. Bob told him you could even fill your engine oil in flight from the front seat, and that Colt was sitting right by the filler. "Wouldn't it spray all over you?" Colt asked. Bob said he didn't know because he has never done it with the engine running.

We took a different route home, and the trip went way too fast. I watched the landscape below me, wondering how much more gold was underneath us. Soon we were landing back in front of our hotel. Stepping out onto our hotel dock, I couldn't believe our luck. This had to be one of our best vacations ever.

A FEW MONTHS went by, and I checked the Discovery Channel show times. I couldn't find an episode about Jack or gold. Maybe it had been shelved. Or maybe I wasn't Googling it right. I tried every imaginable combination for months. Jack Mould-gold-Canada-mines-diamonds-galleon. I keep coming up with was Jack's book,

The Curse of Gold, which I had already ordered and read. The book wasn't written by Jack, but it was about him.

I finally Googled the right combination and this popped up: **"Jack Mould Murdered."**

Wait. What? Murdered?

The article stated that Jack's rifle, some water jugs, and his dog Koti, were found in his pickup a few days after he went missing. One of Jack's boots was found on the shore of the Southgate River. Perhaps he was getting water and slipped in. But a man suspected of his murder was in the Nanaimo jail.

What man? The man who helped us unload the plane? Oh, that poor little dog—he was probably shaking and scared when they found him.

I couldn't believe it. I called up Corilair Flying Service and asked for Bob. Bob came to the phone and said yes, it was true and it is really a shame. Jack had died two weeks after we dropped him off.

Our summer vacation and plane ride took on a new cast. A pall.

Years have gone by, and there is still no trace. I never found out whether the murderer had gone to trial or who he was. Was he the man who helped us unload the plane? Or someone else? Had Jack accidentally slipped into the milky waters of the Southgate River? Who has the gold claim now? Jack said he had a partner, but I've never found anyone who knows any more about his death.

The curse of gold. Jack said he didn't believe in it. I do.

IT'S ALL ABOUT THE FOOD

What do I miss most about flying, other than my airplane? The crew meals.

No, I'm not joking. I loved the crew meals. Not the crew meals on the airplane... the ones on the ground! I miss eating meals with the flight crews on layovers. I've even had fleeting thoughts of hanging out at known crew establishments just to reminisce and pretend I'm still a pilot.

Why was it so much fun? Probably because eating together was the culmination of a long day of weather, mechanical, and passenger problems. We could let down and unwind. We were tired, but we shared the common bond of another successful flight. I especially loved the 'good old days' when we stayed at the same hotels as the flight attendants and all went out together.

Checking into the hotel and figuring out a departure time was always a process. *Ten minutes?* No, twenty. *Twenty?* Yes, to take a shower and change. *Really? I can do it in ten.* Okay, fifteen minutes in the lobby. We would still end up waiting twenty minutes or longer, and the flight attendants always put me to shame when they came down dressed to kill.

Then came the next tough decision. *Where are we eating?* One of the pilots would name a place and the flight attendants would ask, "How far?" *Oh, just a block or so.* Pilot blocks or flight attendant blocks? *Umm. Flight attendant blocks,* the guys would lie. Of course, we pilots always wanted to walk farther because we had been sitting all day. But the joke was that the flight attendants had walked across the entire Pacific Ocean. They just wanted to sit down. We had to compromise by promising to buy dinner, or telling a white lie about how close the restaurant was, to get them to come with us.

When I first started flying internationally I flew all night flights to Europe. All I wanted to do when we landed was go to the hotel and find my bed. The flight attendants told me to go ahead and sleep, but only for a few hours. "Make yourself get up or you won't sleep tonight," they told me. That was the hardest part: getting up. I was groggy because all my body wanted to do was sleep. But I loved walking around Crawley, a little village we stayed in near Gatwick Airport. And I loved going to dinner. The crew always went to *Ye Olde Six Bells*, an old monastery with delicious food. The place was so old that we had to duck to get under the beams on the way to our table. People were shorter in the old days, and the doorways and roofs were lower. The fireplace, though, was big enough to fit a bed in. Good English food sounds like an oxymoron, but I swear it was worth waking up for.

When I began flying to Japan, I was afraid food would be too expensive for my per diem to cover. Osaka wasn't too bad, but I had never been to our hub near Tokyo. I went with the crew to Benihana's on my first night in Narita. Of course it is nicknamed after the famous restaurant chain in the states, and the chef is behind the grill tossing knives. I ordered a plate of noodles and squid for five hundred yen—five dollars back then! Beer was also five hundred yen, but the size of the Sapporo bottle was over three times the size of a regular beer. My worries of food being too expensive were unfounded.

Our favorite spot at the subway station in Osaka was a place called *Twenty-one*. Yes, it is named after the restaurant in New York, but without the celebrity status or the exorbitant prices. Twenty-one is a meal number on the menu. It included an order of gyoza, a huge bowl of noodle soup with pork and sprouts, rice, and a salad. Gyoza is a delicious concoction of pork, cabbage, onions, ginger, garlic, and spices inside a fluted dumpling. It is grilled and served with a dipping sauce of soy and vinegar. For only nine hundred yen, you couldn't beat it for price and taste.

A fluke, you say? How am I ever going to find an obscure restaurant in a foreign subway station? These little mom and pop restaurants are everywhere. You just need to know where to go. Follow the locals… the working-class people. Go to the upper floors of subway stations. Or, better yet, follow a flight crew. We are notoriously cheap.

Most of us can't read Japanese, so we nicknamed the restaurants: *The Red Awning, The Yellow Awning, The Slippery Floor, The Rubber Boot* (the owner wears rubber boots, because the floor is slippery but that adjective was already taken), *The Tonkatsu Place, The Noodle House, The Spiral Staircase,* and *Wendy's* where the food goes around on a conveyor belt and you grab what you want as it goes by.

Wendy's chef

Meals in all of these local dives cost under $10. Octopus salad and yakisoba with squid were two of my favorites. The octopus was a little tricky to eat because the suction cups sometimes stick to the roof of your mouth, and the squid had a different consistency than any other food I had tried, but they were delicious. I even liked eel in my yakisoba. (Don't knock it until you try it!) There are plenty of normal dishes with fish, pork, chicken, or beef if squid, eel, and octopus aren't your cup of tea. You don't have to speak Japanese to eat at local dives, even though the hosts rarely speak English. The

Japanese advertise by placing plastic food outside their establishments in glass cases. If all else failed, we dragged the waiter outside and pointed to the dish we wanted. Losing face is a problem for Asians, but not for us!

One of my favorite restaurants in Osaka was *The Paddle Food Place*. It is a novelty restaurant to us, but quite common in Japan. It was located downstairs in the basement of—you guessed it—a subway station. We ducked under the banners at the front door and were immediately greeted by all the patrons and cooks shouting, *"Irasshaimase!"* loudly and in unison. We answered *"Domo!"* (thank you) because *irasshaimase* means welcome. It was fun because we sat around a horseshoe-shaped table in front of a grill with a chef on the other side. It was different from Benihana's because the food, raw and on ice, was in front of us. We chose our dishes and watched them being cooked. There was so much distance between us and the chef that he had to pass the food out on a long, wooden paddle. At the end of the meal we were charged by the number of empty dishes piled up in front of us. At one dollar per plate, depending on the exchange rate, dinner could be as cheap or expensive as we chose.

Of course, it's possible to spend incredible amounts of money eating in Japan, if one chooses to. My Japanese friends took me out to dinner one night, and the chef was from Osaka and somewhat famous. Each course was an artistic statement, expertly done. The soup arrived with perfectly formed floating shapes. The tofu was served with special garnishes. The fish was concentrically cut, without a nick in the membrane beneath it. The portions were minuscule. Nine courses later, dinner was over and we were still hungry. There were three of us and the bill came to just over three hundred American dollars.

I was shocked. Dinner was good, but not that good. Japanese people often spend that much on dinner. I've heard it is because they don't spend their money on ski boats or luxury items like Americans do, and eating out is their main entertainment. My girlfriend, a native of Japan, didn't consider it worth the price, either.

Another girlfriend and I went to a teahouse in Tokyo in the early nineties. Lunch was forty dollars apiece, I realized after I offered to pay. All we had was yakisoba—a noodle dish with vegetables and squid! Of course, everything in downtown Tokyo was expensive, with lacquer-ware bowls costing four hundred dollars each and clothes triple what they were in the states. A hamburger could cost twenty dollars, and a pizza, thirty or more depending on the toppings.

Cheap breakfasts were a little harder to find, but places do exist. *The Toast Lady* in Osaka was my favorite haunt. The wonderfully kind Japanese owner prepared huge breakfasts of coffee or tea, juice, three eggs, a slice of ham, fried potato cakes, half a banana, half a grapefruit, and stacks of Texas toast... for six hundred yen! You can't get a breakfast like this anywhere else that I know of. We couldn't imagine how she made money, located in the basement of an obscure building with only four tables and a few counter seats. Was she independently wealthy? Did she do this for fun?

The Toast Lady

If so, it was fun for us, too. The walls were covered with pictures of crews, and we recognized most of them. The coffee, tea, and toast were bottomless. You won't find *The Toast Lady* listed in the Yellow Pages. Just follow a flight crew. When we switched hotels to one much farther away, we were devastated. But many of us still made the trek. As I said, we're cheap and we needed the exercise.

My favorite thing to do when I finished eating in Japan was to walk around an outdoor market. Eels and fish were laid out for inspection, a bit like Pike Place Market in Seattle, but with more local flavor and variety. All sorts of strange, odd, and possibly delectable foods surrounded us. The smells assaulted me—some fishy, some spicy, and some pungent. The durian fruit from China was the stinkiest. Northwest Airlines refused to fly it to the United States, even on our freighters. It was described as, "The best custard you will ever eat… in a sewer."

We never knew exactly what we were eating when we were in Asia. I was having dinner at *The Crew Lounge*, a friend's restaurant named for their main patrons—flight crews—in Narita one night. "What is it?" a flight attendant I was with asked.

"I don't know. Fish," I answered. My friend had graciously served us an appetizer for free, and I wasn't about to look a gift horse in the mouth.

"I don't eat anything if I don't know what it is," she said.

What happened to being adventurous and exploring new cultures? Reluctantly, I agreed to ask. I walked over to the small window opening into the kitchen and asked Kazuo what we were eating.

"We call it kinky," he answered in Japanese.

I returned to the table and repeated it, snickering.

"What?" the flight attendant asked incredulously.

"Kinky," I repeated, as the pilots at the next table doubled over laughing. My girlfriend, Akiko, and her sister-in-law asked why that was so funny.

The pilots laughed again. "Let's see you explain this one," they said.

Akiko and I were good friends, so I didn't have any trouble explaining it to her. She had never heard the word kinky, but understood the nuance immediately when I told her what it meant, and repeated it to her sister-in-law in Japanese who burst out laughing and told her husband, Kazuo. The whole restaurant was in on the joke by then, and it was another fun evening in Japan.

I LOVED THE chili crab in Singapore and the nasi goreng in Indonesia, but I wouldn't touch the green eggs in Taipei. I didn't feel great after my meal in Kyoto, either, but it could have been because of the restaurant's health standards. After the meal, the owner's five poodles came in. They urinated on the bar stools before running around in the kitchen to stand on their hind legs, licking the counters. We left quickly, horrified and sick to our stomachs.

One time I was in Thailand at the world's largest outdoor restaurant, Tum Nuk Thai. The menu was fifty-pages-long, including shark fin and other Thai delicacies. The waiters wore roller skates because the place seated three thousand people. It was huge! Their skates clacked on the boards, and the whole place was up on stilts, with dance shows and shops. My girlfriend remarked that there were lots of cats down by the creek underneath us, waiting for scraps. I looked down at the animals. My eyes widened and I told her they definitely 'rhymed' with cats. Thank goodness we had already eaten.

The captain knew of a good restaurant close to the hotel, overlooking an alley in Seoul, Korea. Ordering was iffy, at best, with no plastic food to point to. As we ate our 'mystery meat,' the copilot started making jokes about it being dog. I knew this was a practice in Vietnam, but hadn't given it any thought in Seoul. There weren't any three-legged dogs around, so the captain said we were safe. We all cracked up laughing.

I THINK THAT's what I remember most about my flying career—joking around with the crews. A lot of the guys told great jokes, with accents and punch lines. Some nights I laughed so hard that my stomach hurt the next day. Of course, when I tried to reenact them at home, they were never as funny.

Bangkok was the first place I ever had a shrimp egg
roll with the head, tail, and tentacles still attached.
The antennae got stuck in my throat.

Octopus salad is oishii (delicious).
Use your fingernail to pry the suction cups off
the roof of your mouth.

If you've already eaten something odd,
don't ask what it was.

Drink beer if you don't trust the water. Of course,
formaldehyde is used as a preservative in some Asian
beers, so weigh your choices wisely, Grasshopper.

Akiko and Mitsuo: The salmon at Akos was legendary!

HOTEL ROOM HORRORS

Hotel rooms can be the best or the worst part of traveling. Most of the hotels I stay in are great. Little things may be wrong, but the rooms are clean and comfortable. All hotels are difficult to sleep in during the daytime, even when you've been flying all night and think you can sleep anywhere. I put out my **Do Not Disturb** sign, but it rarely works. The chain clangs against the stop as the maids try to enter. *"Perdón!"* they yell at the top of their voice. So much for sleep.

Tokyo, Japan

THE TWELVE-HOUR PACIFIC Ocean crossing always leaves me exhausted. All I want is my bed, and I'm asleep before my head hits the pillow. I awake a few hours later, terrified and in a panic.

There's someone in my room. I can *feel* his presence. I'm so scared I shake. I keep my eyes closed, pretending to be asleep. He's toying with me, standing at the end of my bed, shaking it. I don't know what to do.

What does he want? How did he get in? Damn. I was so tired when I got to my room that I forgot to look under my bed or check the closet. Did I even lock the door? Did he come through the adjoining door?

I need a weapon. I think of a plan. I can reach the lamp by my bed. If I move fast, I can grab it, throw it at him, and run. *No, I can't.* The lamps in this hotel are attached to the wall. I don't want to be raped or tortured. That's it! The walls are paper-thin. I'll scream!

I scream at the top of my lungs. And yell. Now I've infuriated him. He's shaking the bed harder. This is worse than any nightmare

I've ever had. Wait a minute. Maybe this is a nightmare. No sound came out of my mouth when I screamed...

My brain starts to put everything together. I begin to wake up. The shaking is too violent and rhythmic to be manmade. I open my eyes in the semi-dark room.

There's no one there. Thank God, it's *just* an earthquake. I'm so relieved that I fall back asleep until morning. Down at breakfast I learn the quake was a whopping 6.7 on the Richter scale.

Spokane, Washington

A GIANT SNAKE is strangling me in a jungle monsoon. Gagging, I try to rip him off of me. He only squeezes harder. Panicked, I fight to breathe. Finally, I throw him off and take a deep breath.

Now I'm wide-awake. Turning on the light, I remember where I am. *The Jungle Room.* Who decorated this place? The carpet is bright grassy-green shag. The wallpaper is a shiny foil design with huge, green leaves and bright, orange flowers twisting their way up the walls. The bedspread is a garish orange, and I've tossed and turned and tangled myself tightly in the sheets and bedspread... my giant snake.

I'm soaking wet. The sprinkler system has malfunctioned and everything in the room is drenched, including me. That's my monsoon.

I get up and call the office. I dress, pack, and switch rooms in the middle of the night. The new one is decorated just as badly. There's no telling what my next nightmare will be.

Seoul, Korea and Beijing, China

MY EYES HURT and I can't sleep. The police are trying to break up the student riots down the street with tear gas, and it permeates the air inside. A flight attendant had his suitcase blown up by a Molotov cocktail. I've spent the night waiting for rocks to come flying through my window. This is as bad as being in Beijing, China in the winter, except there it is my throat that burns because China heats with coal. Some winter mornings in Beijing the smog is so thick we can't take off until noon. We only need six hundred feet of forward visibility for our takeoff visibility minimums, but the sun doesn't penetrate until midday.

Chicago, Illinois

ANOTHER DAY, ANOTHER hotel room. Dawn finds me sleeping upright in the armchair wrapped in a blanket cocoon. The mattresses are infested and this is the hotel we refer to as *The Bedbug Inn*. It's hard to sleep when you close your eyes and feel creeping, crawling bugs all over you.

Chino, California

I STARTLE AWAKE. The whole room is shaking. Another earthquake? *No.* There are train tracks right behind the motel and it sounds like the trains are coming through my bathroom window. To make matters worse, the motel is so close to the highway that the semi trucks are shaking the room, too.

The bed crackles as I turn over and try to sleep. *Who puts plastic mattress pads on a bed?* They must rent these rooms to high-class people. When we check out in the morning, the desk clerk has trouble figuring out the cost. It turns out they usually rent the rooms by the hour, not the whole night.

Flying for the Forest Service, we were mapping forest fires all night, trying to sleep during the day. Televisions blared in the rooms around me, and the vacuum cleaners whined as the maids cleaned. Tossing and turning, I somehow managed to get to sleep. *But not for long.*

"Do you think Angie will keep her baby?" one of the cleaning ladies yelled over her vacuum in the room next to me.

"Naw, I'll betcha she has one of those illegal abortions," the other maid answered from the hall.

"Last time she had a baby they made her give it up for adoption."

"No wonder, after she tried to abandon the poor thing. Do you have any more soap? What pig stayed in this room?"

Despite my fatigue, I can't help but listen. I stay as still as possible, trying to hear the rest of the conversation over the whirring of the vacuum.

"Didn't you hear she almost miscarried yesterday after Tony tried to kill her?"

"Lord have mercy! Did they arrest him?"

"With his brother being the chief of police? No way. Besides, this is the third time he tried. They're used to it. Remember the car accident? And that bad fall she had last year?"

"That was Tony?"

"Yep. And his brother knew about it."

What kind of town am I staying in? Are they all crazy?

"Why does she stay with him?"

Why indeed. What a jerk. I can't get back to sleep. I need to report Tony and his brother. And Angie needs long term psychiatric help.

Music plays loudly now, and I'm wide-awake. Again.

One of the maids says, "Look. There's poor Angie now, crying her little heart out."

A soap opera. I feel like an idiot. I get up to take a shower.

The showerhead is set a foot too low, and I ram my head into it. Then I cry out as the water temperature changes to scalding hot.

I'm guessing someone flushed a toilet up above me. How in the hell can I stay awake to fly all night tonight?

Luxury

LATELY I'VE SPENT fewer nights in the mildew manors of the world. My international travels have taken me to a new level of expectation. Decorated with gorgeous silk curtains and beautiful oriental-print duvets, the rooms are large and spacious. The furniture is teak, and the bathrooms have marble tubs and floors. Hot tea, baskets of fresh fruit, and orchids await me. The bed is turned down at night, and there are mints and a fresh orchid on the pillow.

Expectations are easily dashed. If the hotels are overbooked in Japan, they send us to another hotel with rooms the size of a closet. Often we have to wait hours for our rooms to be ready after flying all night. We arrive so early that most guests haven't checked out yet, and there are no clean, empty rooms. Guests have to check out and maids need to clean. Meanwhile we sit in the lobby, too exhausted to do anything else.

Singapore

I CAN SLEEP in the middle of any airport, dead to the world, while public address systems blare and people yell into their cell phones. I can sleep on the floor of a freighter as the loaders slam boxes around below and groomers vacuum around me. I can sleep through ice machines plinking ice, elevators dinging, drunks singing in the hall, and heavy street noise. *Why can't I sleep now, when I have to fly in four hours?*

There's an argument in the next room. A lady is screaming at her boyfriend to "Get the f*** out." He doesn't want to leave. He begs her to let him stay. He loves her. He just wants to be with her. It's two in the morning for God's sake.

I'm not mad anymore. But it is hard to hear the whole conversation, so I grab a drinking glass and press it against the wall, mashing my ear onto it. The argument goes on for twenty minutes. Unfortunately, security arrives before I can figure the whole story out, and the boyfriend is led away in protest, still pleading his love. Laughing, I pack and get ready for the day. I head down to the lobby for coffee and pastries.

The flight engineer is already downstairs. He was in the room on the other side of the feuding couple. He says the girlfriend is a pornographic movie star from California. Her boyfriend was turned on watching the filming, and he couldn't leave her alone. I add the part I heard. "She was just tired and wanted to sleep. They had had sex seven times already and he still wanted more." We double over laughing, comparing notes.

Just then the captain comes downstairs. He yells at the front desk clerk, the same lady who has already apologized to us over and over. We try to calm him down, and explain what was going on. He's mad at us for laughing, but we can't stop. We keep remembering more details. Here we are, thousands of miles from home, having the best entertainment we've had in a long time.

New York, New York

FINALLY, I'M SPENDING the night in a hotel that is famous and prestigious. I've seen advertisements for this hotel on television and the rooms looked amazing. The location is great, too. It's close to Times Square, and good restaurants, world class shopping, and theaters surround it. The lobby is unbelievable, with deep plush carpeting and huge chandeliers hanging from the ceiling. *Yes. This is my kind of hotel.* People in fur coats, elegant gowns, and tuxedos surround me. A bellman accompanies me upstairs, unlocks the door, and carries the bags into my room.

Wait. There must be some mistake. This room is hundreds of dollars a night, yet it is smaller than a walk-in closet. There is no floor space because the tiny bed takes up the entire room. Under the mirrored ceiling, two walls are covered with bright, fuzzy-red and silver-foiled wallpaper patterned with diamonds. The other two are mirrored, in a pathetic attempt to create an illusion of space. *So much for advertising.* Discouraged, I tip the bellman and deadbolt the door behind him. I remove the bedspread and plunk down on the bed. It's as hard as a rock.

I turn on the television and hear the passion before I see it. A pornographic channel. Quickly I switch it off. *Great. Just Great.* Opening the curtains, I look out my window directly into another window less than five feet away. There is a man in a dirty white T-shirt drinking a beer, belching loudly as he watches his television. *What a dump.*

Later I learned the hotel had hidden cameras in the rooms recording sexual escapades and trysts. One of our captains saw himself on the porno channel with his wife.

Dallas, Texas

THE DOORKNOB FELL off in my hand when I tried to enter my hotel room. Trudging back to the front desk, the clerk didn't even blink an eye as I handed him the doorknob. He gave me another key, and I dragged my bags to the new room. The doorknob worked, but the windows were filthy and I couldn't see out of them. I was too tired to complain, so I went to bed.

Narita Japan had a spring-fed pool that was freezing cold.

I loved the Manila Hotel pool on the harbor with the swim up bar.

Kansas City, Kansas

SOME NIGHTS, WHEN I'm jet lagged and exhausted and the key card won't work in the door and I have to drag my bags all the way back to the lobby, I just want to cry. Sometimes the room is occupied, and not just with someone else's belongings. I opened the door one night and there was a half-naked guy lying on the bed. He was snoring loudly, wearing only his underwear and cowboy boots. He was cute, but I quickly backed out the door.

The desk clerk was very apologetic. "I'm so sorry. The Dallas Cowboys are here and I gave you one of their rooms by mistake."

Damn. Maybe I should have kept that room. It gets lonely on the road, miles away from everyone you love. If you can't be with the ones you love, love the ones you're with, right? *Can I have that key back, please?*

Miami, Florida

ANOTHER DAY, ANOTHER city. I'm alone in the cockpit, doing my preflight. A flight attendant comes up to say hello and to tell me she is deadheading. Her voice is weary and shaking. I ask her what's wrong. She sighs, drops into the jumpseat, and tells me her story.

"I stepped into the elevator this morning and pushed the button for the lobby. As the doors closed, I realized I wasn't alone. A big rat was trapped in the elevator with me. He was huge—two feet long at least, not including his tail. I started screaming, and the rat freaked out. He started running up the wall. When he got to the top, he fell to the floor, onto my feet. I screamed louder. I couldn't reach the elevator buttons without stepping on the rat. Over and over he tried to run up the wall, falling back down as I shrieked. At last the doors opened into the lobby and I stumbled out and fainted.

Meanwhile, the elevator went back up to pick up another flight attendant. The rat ran out over her feet and down the hall. She was still screaming when she got to the lobby. People surrounded me, as I was lying on the floor. The front desk clerk was leaning over me, trying to calm me down. 'It was just a leetle mouse, yes?' he kept saying, over and over.

I lost it and grabbed him by his tie. Yanking his face close to mine, I yelled, 'No, it was not a leetle mouse. It was a huge, fucking, rat, over two feet long. Get it?'"

"He got it," she said, shaking her head.

I stared at her with my mouth open. Now that's a bad day. I repeated her story to the guys I was flying with when they finished flight planning. They thought their stories were worse:

Fort Lauderdale, Florida

"SOMETHING WAS CRAWLING on me in the middle of the night," the captain said. "When I turned on the light, a nine-inch long cockroach was sitting on my chest, looking at me, waving his antennae. I tried to grab it, but he jumped off the bed. I chased it across the room and beat it to death with my shoe, until the white stuff gushed out. Then I put it in the trashcan, so I could show the hotel manager what a dump he had. But by morning it was gone.

"That got me thinking. *Did it crawl off in pieces or did something bigger eat it?* Things to ponder alone in the dark.

"We switched hotels, from the *Cockroach Castle* to the *Mildew Manor*. The new one wasn't much better," the captain finished.

Montego Bay, Jamaica

"THAT'S NOTHING," THE copilot said, one-upping him. "I woke up in pain down in Montego Bay. My arm was throbbing. Man, it hurt. The sheets were sticky and I had trouble freeing my arm to reach for the light. There was a something in bed with me. A rat! Chewing on my arm. There was blood all over my bed. I had to go to the hospital and get stitches."

"What about rabies? Weren't you worried?" I asked.

"Of course I was, but the doctors and nurses told me Jamaica is a rabies-free country. I'm not dead yet, and that was a few years ago."

The captain and I looked at each other, open-mouthed. As bad as his story was, this last story from a flight attendant wins the prize.

San Francisco, California

"I WAS EXHAUSTED after walking across the Pacific Ocean. All I wanted was to take a shower and go to bed. The smell hit me like a wave when I opened my door. The room smelled awful. I couldn't even go in. When I got back to the front desk, the desk clerk said they were completely full. He sent housekeeping up with me to check out the room. I didn't think anything would help, but I was too tired to fight with him.

"We opened the door and housekeeping started spraying pine tree air freshener all over. The smell disappeared. Now the room smelled like a forest. A fresh, pine forest. It was much better. I nodded and thanked her, and she left the air freshener can with me, just in case I needed it later.

"I jumped into the shower. When I was done, I reached for the towel and almost keeled over. The smell was back. Holding my nose, spraying air freshener, I dripped to the phone. This time I insisted they send the manager.

"The manager gagged when I opened the door to let him in. He checked inside the closet, behind the curtains, and under the bed. *There was a dead body under the bed.* He called the cops.

"Apparently, three days earlier, the previous occupant never checked out. The maids packed up his belongings, cleaned the room, and made the bed. They never noticed the man had been murdered and stuffed under the bed. *It happens.*

"The hotel really was full. The only open room was the penthouse suite. *I deserved it.* Six rooms on the top floor of the hotel, with a dining room table that seated twelve. It had a full kitchen with a washer, a dryer, and a dishwasher. There was a killer stereo system, and a big living room with knickknacks and art, because people who stay in penthouses probably don't steal stuff like that. Or they can afford to pay for it if they do.

"I wandered around, too revved up to sleep. I couldn't get the thoughts in my head to shut off. I even checked under the bed. Twice. There weren't even any dust-bunnies under it. But every time I closed my eyes, all I could think about was that dead body."

Never forget to check under the bed.

ENGLAND OR HONG KONG?

When we flew to London, pilots and flight attendants complained that our layover village of Crawley, near Gatwick, was too small and isolated. Northwest Orient Airlines moved us to Brighton Beach instead. I liked Crawley, but I loved being near an ocean. Brighton was usually cold, gray, and rainy, but so is the Oregon Coast. I'd drag my jetlagged self out of bed, grab my book and an umbrella, and walk the quaint, winding streets of Brighton. The little shops with their lace and old postcards were fascinating, and I spent hours window shopping. The Royal Pavilion was in the center of Brighton, and I never tired of looking at its domes and minarets. My favorite places to go were the pubs. Sitting by the fire, listening to the English accents while I read my book and drank my pint of beer, made me feel like I was in a storybook of old. The regulars looked at me like I had three heads, but I pretended not to notice. I whiled away the hours and watched their world go by as they greeted one another and drank a bit. My heart was singing as I walked back to my hotel from my mini-vacation days.

It wasn't a long trip to Dover and when it was good weather, it was fun to go out on the long pier and look toward the white cliffs. After all, I was born in Dover, Delaware. On the beach, there were very few shells, but there were cuttlefish skeletons everywhere. It was so strange to see what I had always called "parakeet chews"—what caged birds sharpen their beaks on—and learn they were bones from a squid-like fish. The arcade on the pier was another treat, and I learned to snare toys after talking to the man who restocked the machines. One time my suitcase home was full of mini soccer balls!

The English are not known for good food, but I loved *Sweet Tibby Dunbar's* in Portland, Oregon and looked forward to prime rib and popovers in England. Imagine my surprise when, instead, I found Indian restaurants everywhere in England. Indian food became something I looked forward to, especially Tandoori chicken and naan. Fish and chip places were everywhere, too, and I loved eating it with malted vinegar. English food never disappointed me.

Sometimes I would take the train to nearby castles, like Arundel and Lewes, or travel to Alfriston and Horsham to see cottages and churches. I never made it to Bodiam Castle—everyone's favorite.

Most of the trips from my West Coast base took me to Asia instead of Europe. I missed England, but Hong Kong became one of my favorite layovers—once I got over the culture shock. I still heard English accents in Hong Kong, and visited the pubs, but the similarities ended there.

The first time we headed into Hong Kong from the airport, the captain I was with had to shush me when I was exclaiming about the poverty. He didn't want me to insult the van driver. We stayed at the *Holiday Inn Golden Mile* hotel in Kowloon, near the famous *Bottoms Up Club* of 007 James Bond fame. The sidewalks were full of gold and opulence, but the living conditions above the shops and the areas around the hotel were disheartening.

Rule number one in Hong Kong's Kowloon district: Don't open your curtains. The apartment buildings were so close to our hotel that I could almost touch them. I never knew what I would experience looking out my window. One time a man was belching and farting with the television blaring. Another time there were piles of jeans with five people sleeping on them and one person sewing. The dark, dirty alleys were bad enough, but the rickety scaffolding and gray laundry hanging on antennas was depressing. People dropped things out their windows, so there was trash and dirty laundry all over the roofs and air conditioners. I learned to keep my curtains closed and live in the fake opulent hotel-world of teak, marble, and silk.

Some layovers I would catch the Star Ferry over to Hong Kong Island, then a bus to Stanley Market from Central. Sitting in the open air, up on the top level of the double-decker bus, I knew I was taking my life into my hands. Some of the corners were treacherous on the narrow road. I held my hands up or ducked as branches crashed into the side of the bus and my face, and closed my eyes as oncoming traffic crossed over the centerline. There was always an accident on the way. A sign outside the tunnel illuminated Hong Kong deaths from traffic accidents—over 20,000 people by the end of one year!

One night, when I tried to get the guys to go out for a beer, they turned me down because they were tired. I was shocked. No one goes right to bed in Hong Kong unless they're sick. I pushed relentlessly, but the answer was a firm no. Undeterred, I headed out on my own after changing into my jeans. As I walked out of the hotel I couldn't help but notice two Americans ahead of me on the sidewalk. It was the captain and copilot. *Damn them, they were ditching me!* I followed at a safe distance and saw them head down the stairs into *Bottoms Up*. I laughed to myself and kept walking.

The next day, flying back to Narita, Japan, I prodded them a bit. "I can't believe you two wouldn't go out last night. It was a perfect temperature to take a walk and grab a beer." They glanced at each other, but stuck to their rehearsed line, "We were too tired."

"But not too tired for a drink at *Bottoms Up?*"

They looked at each other and cracked up. "Busted," they said in unison.

Our next crew hotel was The Park Lane on Hong Kong Island. Looking out my new hotel window onto Victoria Park was much better. There were always exhibits on display, people practicing Tai Chi, or the famous Cirque de Soleil set up in the park. The mountains, water, and architecture of Hong Kong somehow make up for the crowding and poverty. Parts of Hong Kong are just beautiful, and the new hotel made it even easier to go to Stanley Market.

The view from the yacht club facing Kowloon was nice, but the harbor water was disgusting. Sometimes I just walked around the harbor looking at the junks and freighters. But the smell was so overpowering with the floating debris that I never stayed too long.

Smugglers in Hong Kong

Ye Old Six Bells in England

I don't think this is what Hong Kong's name, Fragrant Harbor, really means. It seemed so easy to clean it when the wind is blowing and all the debris rests against the retainer wall, but no one ever does. If only I had a giant strainer…

The large, floating restaurant in Aberdeen was closed whenever I tried to go there, but at least I got to see it even if I couldn't eat there. I loved getting off the double-decker bus at Ocean Park, about halfway to Stanley. Ocean Park is an amusement park that is so huge that it goes over a mountain and down the other side. It encompasses everything from Chinese history to sea life and rides. They had a reef exhibit that was incredible—an island with a palm tree that you walked around, looking at fish through the glass underneath. First you saw small, colorful, tropical fish on a barrier reef, and then somehow you spiraled down, down, down into the depths of the ocean, encountering bigger fish and different species all the way. The fish grew larger and less colorful, and then there were just sharks. I never went on the roller coaster, because it looked scary as hell, dipping out over the South China Sea. But I loved taking the cable cars, bobbing over the water and fishing boats on the two-mile trip.

Going by the different beaches on the way to Stanley and looking at the mansions along the way was a completely different experience from the downtown slums of Hong Kong. Stanley is on a hillside at the end of the bus line. The dark, tiny shops of the market are full of finds, like Tommy Bahama tops and Greg Norman golf shirts for seven dollars. It's easy to get lost inside the maze, but you always break out eventually, and you can see the water and get your bearings.

The beach at Stanley couldn't be more different than the beach in England. It was rocky, and there were junks and fishing boats with islands in the distance. The *Boat House Restaurant* was a great place to read my book and eat French cuisine while overlooking the South China Sea on their third story deck. The weather in Hong Kong was much nicer than the weather in England.

I liked an English bar on the waterfront called *Smugglers*, too.

The monks and tourists walking by were different, but the similarities didn't escape my notice. The bartenders had the same English accents, and the fish and chips were just as greasy as the ones at Brighton Beach. I knew I wasn't in jolly old England when I paid for my food and drink in Hong Kong dollars. There was money from all over the world stapled to the ceiling, and the atmosphere was raucous. For years I wrote my Christmas cards at *Smugglers*, getting the photos printed for cheap in the nearby market as I watched Mr. Bean on the television and drank my pint of beer.

The culture in Hong Kong is variable. High-tech high-rises are set next to old-style fishing boats. There's gold and affluence on the street level, but poverty on the floors above. We stayed near the noonday gun now that we were on the island, so I had to be prepared not to jump out of my skin as I was walking by it when it went off. Sometimes I just walked the streets looking at everything for sale. I stuck with the flight attendants to buy jewelry, because they were experts on buying pearls and gold. There were giant open-air markets selling everything from cheap clothes and jewelry to pirated software. I always bought too much, and sometimes I had to buy an extra suitcase to get it all home.

Riding the ferries to outlying islands was always fun. The views couldn't be beat, and it gave me a whole new perspective of Hong Kong. One time I went to Cheung Chou, a nearby island with a monastery and bike paths. The Cheung Chou VOR (radio station) was a navigation aid on our approach plates, and I wanted to see what was underneath me flying in. I met a busboy on the ferry, and we talked about life in Hong Kong. He told me about a man who couldn't swim and tried to commit suicide the month before by jumping off the Star Ferry. The man was rescued and resuscitated, but he still died ten days later from the infections he acquired by drinking the polluted water. The busboy was on the same ferry hours later when I went back, and he showed me some great places to eat in Central, including the restaurant he worked at. He was Australian, and was leaving soon because he feared the handover coming up on July 1, 1997, when British rule ended.

One layover I went to Lantau Island, long before the new airport was built. It was horrible weather, with the rain pouring down in sheets, but I wanted to see the giant Buddha. I had to be careful climbing the slippery steps. Asian stone steps are carved by hand, and sometimes the treads are different heights, so you have to be extra careful. I looked and felt like a drenched rat, but it was worth the trip to the top!

I heard there were pink dolphins, also called Chinese white dolphins, living in the water surrounding Lantau. I signed up for a tour on my next trip in. They really were pink! There are only a few populations of pink dolphins in the world—the Pearl River Delta and the Amazon River. Scientists think they are pink because their blood vessels are near the surface to let off heat in the tropical waters, but don't really consider them a separate species. A pink bottlenose has even been spotted in Louisiana. Unfortunately, their habitat is disappearing with landfill at the same time it is being polluted. I wanted to see them before they were all gone.

These dolphins can live in the turbid, muddy, delta waters, but they can't survive the pollution in the South China Sea near Hong Kong and Macau. Their life span is down to twenty years. With births occurring every four to five years, they are not repopulating fast enough. To make matters worse, their first baby almost always dies. Whether the dolphin's environment is toxic, or whether their body can't handle their first pregnancy, no one knows.

The international flight attendants told me about losing their first baby when they found out I was pregnant. They said it was common, and not to worry, because it is nature's way of keeping the healthiest babies. Sure enough, I lost one of the twins I was carrying right after a trip to Asia and back. I quit flying for the rest of my pregnancy and had a healthy baby boy.

I always had a plan when my next month's schedule included a Hong Kong layover. There were so many corners of the colony I had yet to see, and the flight attendants and pilots always knew of someplace new. For years, I wanted to ride the tram to Victoria's Peak, but it was always foggy. I waited and waited, until finally the weather cooperated. I took the bus to Central with another pilot, and rode the tram at last. What a view! What a life!

Grow where you are planted. Love where you are at.

CASTLES IN JAPAN

When I first started flying to England, I would set out to see the nearest castle if the weather was good. Flying to Osaka, Japan, the thought of visiting a castle wasn't even on my radar, as we pilots say. Then the captain and copilot took me to a vodka bar one night with an astounding view of the Osaka Castle. They sipped expensive vodka poured over ice cubes chipped off a huge block of ice. I don't like vodka, but looking at the huge, lighted castle was incredible.

I walked there the next day. Our hotel was only a mile away, but the castle was hidden by tall buildings. I wasn't positive I was headed in the right direction. Then I round a corner and the castle of Shogun fame appeared before me. It was just as impressive in the light. There was a park around it, and the air was full of insects screeching. Kids were armed with nets and boxes, and one grandfather was showing his grandson how to catch the cicadas. Entranced, I paused and watched.

The imposing structure dwarfed everything around it, and I couldn't wait to see inside. I paid the money to enter and crossed the moat on the bridge. Disappointment struck as I stepped inside. The castle was just a shell—a concrete reproduction of the marvelous castle that was once on this very spot. It's just a museum, with no grand rooms, and no one has ever lived in it. I went back outside and started reading *Shogun* by James Michener.

There was something about reading *Shogun* here that made the location even more compelling. The place came alive on the pages, and the characters seemed more real in the castle's shadow. I decided to read the book only at the castle, on my layovers. Flying out of Los Angeles, Osaka was our only international destination in the late 1980s, so I finished the book in a couple of months.

I couldn't wait to see more of Japan, and not just castles. At first the subway was daunting, with all the Japanese writing and symbols everywhere. Then I realized there was one English sign in every station. As long as I knew which direction I was going, I could count stops. I took a train to Nara, to see the deer park, and it was easy. The deer were everywhere, and the vendors were friendly, even if they didn't speak English.

I flew a trip with a group of flight attendants who were going to Kyoto to see the temples and castles. They invited me along. Halfway through the first castle, Nijo, I realized I was with a bunch of nuts. Los Angeles flight attendants were so much fun! The temple had squeaky floors to warn its occupants of intruders, and one of the guys started making creaky noises. Soon we were all cracking up. This continued all day, from Nijo, to Kinkaku-ji, to the Ryoanji. Sitting on the wall outside the Ryoanji Temple, looking into the garden of perfectly raked sand, we were supposed to be reverent. One of the guys whispered, "Look, that ant is stealing the sand! Put it back, you!" He points to the imaginary ant that we all pretend we can see and once again, the silence was shattered. We couldn't stop laughing.

MASSAGE, AAHH!

It had been a few years since I'd been to Bangkok, Thailand. You could still cut the smog with a butter knife, and I never liked the crowding, the traffic, or the smell of sewage. But I still loved Bangkok. Being in Thailand always took me back to the stories of Siam that I read as a child. I never dreamed I would get to go there someday, especially not routinely.

DAN, THE SECOND officer, wants to go to Wat Poh. Wat Poh is a temple famous for having the largest horizontal Buddha in the world. It's a huge, gold reclining statue with gigantic golden toes. I stare at the toes for a long time, either amazed or jet lagged... some days I'm not sure which. We make our way through the temple, past monks and tourists, to a large, open-air room in the middle of the courtyard. *This is why we are here: The Massage School.*

For 300 baht, about eleven dollars, we can get a one-hour massage with herbs and a clean sheet. I turn down the herbs, because I don't want my skin to be yellow all day like it was last time. Besides, I like the pressure massage without a burning hot bag of herbs. I change into a safflower-colored tunic and brown pants that they provide in a little curtained room. They are huge on me. Walking out, my masseuse, Awho, adjusts them, laughing. I didn't know they were supposed to tie. Awho looks like a young boy, but he's probably much older. I'm terrible at guessing ages of Asians because they all look younger than we do for our age.

Lying on a thin mattress, I hear the monks walking by, humming and chanting. Temple bells gong and echo in the distance.

Awho knows pressure points very well, I decide, as my cares melt away. Thais are masters at their craft and they use their whole body to massage you. Their feet are an integral part of the massage, and Awho turns me into putty within minutes.

The room is large. There are twenty or more masseuses on our side of the room alone. Dan is on one side of me and some guy with lots of tattoos is on my other side. The temperature is over one hundred degrees, and the humidity is almost as high. A fan is above me, so it feels cool. I can't understand a word of Thai, and it doesn't feel crowded with my eyes closed.

I helped these monks with their English in exchange for their picture!

WHEN I MENTION Thai massage, my girlfriends back home ooh and aah. It's a treat, something they do once a year. To me it's a necessity, and a small price to pay for sanity, stress reduction, and health. I get them all the time. Traveling to Asia all these years has taught me to be more relaxed and less self-conscious. I used to worry about whether to leave my clothes on or off. I worried about my birthmarks, my stretch marks, my cellulite, or any other body fault I could conjure up.

The first time I had a professional massage, I took off my shirt and pants but left my underwear on. The second time I had just been for a swim, and my suit was damp. My masseuse told me she could do a better job if I took everything off. So, I took a deep breath and complied. After all, a good masseuse keeps you covered up on the table, to keep you warm and protect your modesty. Still, it was a huge step for me. I've since decided I was being foolish. I leave my inhibition at the door or forever miss the enjoyment of a great massage.

When I'm in a private room with my clothes off, I choose a female masseuse. At the temple, wearing a pair of shorts and shirt, it doesn't matter as much. Except that sometimes guys push too hard for me. I know, male masseuses are supposed to be sexy and all, but I'm not as comfortable with them as I am with women. It probably has to do with a few bad experiences. One time, in Manila, the ladies at the spa told me the pool cleaner was giving me my massage. I told them, *No!* They were surprised, because he told them I asked for him. *No I did not!* Another time a Singaporean masseuse made me uncomfortable and tried to give me a "happy ending" massage. *Hell no!*

In Korea, they train the blind to give massage. Your masseuse is escorted to your hotel room. The first time I ordered a massage in my room I thought, *There's no need to worry about body faults with her since she can't see.* I was wrong. Navigating the room, and my body, with ease, she remarked, "Ahh, you have child?" as her fingers coursed my stretch marks. Later, as she massaged my hips, she said, "You are very tiny except down here." After that I was almost more inhibited than with a seeing masseuse!

I OPEN MY eyes when I hear a gong, and see the monks walking by, chanting. Glancing upward, the gold spires and orange tiled roofs seem dream-like. Thai temples are amazing, and the monks are friendly. Sometimes they just want to practice their English, and I love talking with them. Now all the masseuses are singing quietly in Thai. The peaceful chanting takes me away, along with my aches and pains.

Dan and I decide to stay for an extra hour. Dan is thrilled to find someone who loves long massages as much as he does. He was eating at a Mexican restaurant in the States when a huge beam fell on his shoulder. It was luck, he says, that it hit him and missed his infant niece in her car seat by inches. He says this is the only place in the world where he can find relief from his pain without drugs.

Later Dan tells me there were beggars looking in, asking for money. I'm glad I had my eyes closed and never saw them.

I'm glad to be back in Bangkok.

SHOPPING IN SEOUL

Why does anyone go to Korea? To shop, of course. Especially around Christmas, Seoul is the place to go. Years ago, before the Seoul Olympics, prices were much cheaper in Itaewon, but there are still deals to be had if you know how to bargain.

Need a designer bag at a bargain basement price? Just tell the shopkeeper what you need and he will run out the door, down the alley, maybe to his house... and come back with it! I was looking for a designer Dalmatian purse for my sister-in-law that was $2000 back home. It was a brand-new, coveted design that was very hard to find. I searched and searched, and was directed here and there. Sure enough, it was behind a couch in a secret compartment in one of the shops. My sister-in-law had helped my mom through knee surgeries and breast cancer and I owed her. I was a hero that Christmas.

Sometimes things are knockoffs, and sometimes they are real. Need a ski coats for $20? Reebocks and Nike shoes for $7? You have to know your products, and you have to shop with savvy flight attendants. Designer sweaters, hats, suitcases, dresses, shirts, stuffed animals, scarves, baby clothes—you name it, you can find it if you know where to look. And it is all amazingly cheap, starting at a buck or two. *Dollars.* The Koreans always want American cash if possible.

Koreans are masters at copying anything. Filipinos shine at imitating our musicians. Both Koreans and Filipinos can embroider and sew. Some of the guys call Korea the "land of the almost right." They aren't trying to be cruel—they have gotten home and had one leg or sleeve shorter than the other, or the size was off, or the spelling. You have to be observant, and try things on. Let the buyer beware.

I think the real fun is the bargaining and the amount of goods for sale crammed into such a small shopping area. Itaewon is the famous place to shop for bargains, and every hotel has a bus that goes there. I used to come back with a suitcase that weighed a

Shopping in Asia is all about the sights and smells. And the deals!

ton. Or I would buy an extra suitcase. I brought ski coats back for everyone I know, as well as shoes, stuffed animals, and sweaters. The best part of the shopping was the show and tell on the bus to the hotel, or the airplane on the way home.

"What? How did I miss that?"

"How much did you pay? $15? You got ripped off big time. I got it for $10."

"Oh my gosh, that's beautiful I'll have to get it next time!"

How do you get through customs with so much crap? As long as you are honest about what you are bringing back, you are usually okay. Don't get greedy and bring back too much, and don't sell it in the States. Customs officials told us not to put them in a bind by getting too detailed about what we had. They told us to list things on the form without brand names: 7 golf shirts, 5 purses. Not: 7 Greg Norman logo golf shirts, 3 Dooney & Bourke purses, 2 Gucci bags. One official told me, "We don't want to know!"

I talked to some of the representatives for the companies who were on our flights. Their consensus was that it was part of the cost of doing business outside the United States in a place that had different laws. They knew about the fakes, and even let the employees take home some of the real merchandise, as a perk. Advertising, they called it, laughing. Besides, one of the designer purse representatives said, the fakes aren't real gold and they fall apart.

The older I got, the more my conscience kicked in, especially with computer programs, music, and movies. We have copyright laws for a reason. I was more careful what I bought and where. Besides, I was never crazy about designer-anything, except as a joke. The hoity-toity life style, caring what people think or imitating a Kardashian, wasn't for me.

Korea wasn't the only place I shopped, of course. Beijing became a favorite spot for clothes and pearls. Hong Kong was great for jewelry, clothes, and video games. The Duty Free store was great for cheap liquor. I shopped for distraction, not need. I found inexpensive Lilliput and David Winter collector houses in England at Duty Free. I liked tiny pewter figurines, and I could buy them in

Singapore for a song. It was like a treasure hunt, and it gave me a mission—a way to break up a long trip away from home.

My only problem with customs was over something stupid. Persimmons. My girlfriend in Japan, Akiko, gave me two persimmons she grew in her yard, so we could share them on the way home in the cockpit. We had an emergency on the way home, and we were so busy that I forgot about the fruit. When I put my bag on the belt in Seattle, guess what showed up? The custom's lady literally started screaming at me. "You flight attendants do this all the time. I'm sick of it. Each violation is $250. You have two." I tried to explain. She kept yelling. I was mortified. Twenty minutes later, she was still on me, livid that I dared try to smuggle in fruit. I finally said, "Fine, fine me. I don't care. I just want to go home." A male customs agent came over and settled her down. "It's almost Christmas. Let her go," he said. "You've badgered her enough."

Staying calm in the face of chaos usually works.

VOLCANO VACATION

The first time I went to Seoul, Korea, in 1988, I was not impressed. It was smoggy, cold, rainy, and we were stuck in traffic on the way to the hotel. The city was dirty and the river was disgusting. But I learned to enjoy my layovers there, just as I had learned to enjoy my Hong Kong layovers.

A few years after the Olympics, I bid a schedule that flew between Seoul and Manila for an entire week. I was the flight engineer on our Boeing 747/200, Dave Mathison was the copilot, and our captain was Neil Atkinson. We were good friends after flying together the month before. Neil's wife, Cathy, was sitting in first class. Neil was turning sixty and this was his last trip, a reluctant celebration of sorts. Retirement was mandatory, and Neil was in a much better mood than he had been on our last flight.

The month before, while we were flying in Asia, Cathy bought a two-million-dollar condominium building in Newport, Oregon. Neil hadn't seen the property, and he was not happy to have that much of *his* money spent without his approval. Dave and I consoled him for days as he ranted. But when Neil went home after the trip, he flew out to see the condominium and loved it. It was called Starfish Point. It had six individual units, plus a separate office and apartment for the managers. The units were multi-leveled with sunken living rooms, fireplaces, and Jacuzzi tubs. The views were incredible, and the two-bedroom units had multiple balconies. Now Neil couldn't wait to start fixing it up and he had something to look forward to in retirement. Neil decided Starfish Point was worth every cent his wife and son had spent.

Waking up in Korea the first morning, I had a surprise call from crew scheduling. Our flight was cancelled. Mount Pinatubo was erupting. Aircraft engines are dangerously susceptible to ash, as are our airframes and windows. Our company made the decision to cancel all flights into Manila until the volcano calmed down.

We were thrilled! Having a paid vacation was not something any of us were expecting. Cathy wanted to shop for treasures to put in the gift shop at Starfish Point, so we all went to Itaewon on our first day off. Cathy ended up spending $10,000 on antique furniture. The shop owner was thrilled, and proclaimed he was her long-lost brother. He offered to chauffeur us around Korea. The next day, when our flight was cancelled again, he drove us to a Korean folk village south of Seoul.

Driving in his Mercedes, chatting along the way, we learned and saw things we never could have known as mere tourists. As we walked around the folk village, it seemed like a fantasy world, with a wedding ceremony and exhibits. Cathy's "brother" admitted it brought back bad memories for him. He had grown up in a similar village and never wanted to be that poor ever again.

On the way back to Seoul, we were caught in a three-hour traffic jam next to a truckload of chickens. The smog and heat were horrible on this summer day in June of 1991, and one by one the chickens keeled over and died. We joked that somewhere, at some restaurant that night, those chickens would not go to waste. I never ordered chicken in Seoul after that.

Dave and Neil were ex-military, so we went to the military base for dinner. There were many choices there. We ate at the English pub one night, the pizza joint the next, and the French restaurant the third night. The only problem was that at the French restaurant, jackets were required. Dave didn't have one. The maître d' suggested he use mine. My new, white-linen jacket came to Dave's elbows and I threatened him with his life if he ripped it. He looked like Don Johnson off of Miami Vice, and we teased him mercilessly. The food was delicious, and Neil was sure this was the best trip of his career.

Cathy and I got along famously. Everyone thought we were mother and daughter, so we got a lot of mileage out of that, too. For seven days, we did whatever we wanted to, because every morning we would call crew schedules to make sure we were still not going to fly to Manila. Cathy filled the drawers of her furniture with stuffed animals—real deals in Itaewon. She negotiated a "great" price only to find that I had beaten her price by a dollar or so on my animals. I bought a huge stuffed monkey that my neighbor wanted for $7, but Cathy had paid $9. So, she marched back to the vendor in her tough negotiator mode and bought more monkeys for $6 apiece. We laughed about that in later years when we reminisced.

Dave and I went to Lotte World one day by ourselves, to give Neil and Cathy some time alone. Lotte makes chewing gum, and all the kids back home in Sherman County, Oregon where I live begged me to bring back Lotte gum. They had blueberry, mangosteen, and green apple—flavors we didn't have yet in the states.

Lotte World looked a lot like Disneyland, with its rides and castle, except there were raccoons as mascots instead of mice. Dave and I towered over the Koreans, and our light-brown hair stood out in the crowd of black-haired locals. We laughed when Lorry and Lotty, the raccoons, came running over to get their pictures taken with us. We rode the rides and watched the parades feeling like pseudo-celebrities, and had a blast.

The next day I met a friend of my father-in-law's for lunch. He showed me how delicious Korean barbecue was and where to get it near our hotel. I loved the little grills in the center of the tables, and how you wrapped your meat in lettuce after you cooked it. Another night I was treated to dinner by the Lees, a family I had met on a flight the month before, and they opened my eyes to how delicious all Korean food was—even smelly kimchee!

By the end of the week, the volcano was still blowing up, but the company pulled the plug on our vacation. It was an amazing seven days, and I had learned to love Korea, even though it was locked in smog the entire time we were there. I don't know how they got the air cleaned up for the Olympics three years earlier, but it was back to dirty now.

I loaded my monkey into the cockpit jump seat with his oxygen mask on, a seatbelt, and peanuts. It was a bittersweet flight home.

I never saw Dave again, not even at the Sport's Bar in Narita, but I never forgot the fun week we had. At least I saw Neil and Cathy for years to come, as Starfish Point became our favorite place on the Oregon Coast. We even rented it for our daughter's wedding. I always enjoyed the gift shop, and there were still a few pieces of Korean furniture fifteen years later.

Volcanoes can be a good thing.

TUNNELS BENEATH NORTH KOREA

The only thing we really wanted to do but couldn't while Mount Pinatubo was blowing its stack was go to the DMZ between North and South Korea. The government needed our passports for a day before they would let us go there, and we never knew for sure if we would be flying the next day, so we couldn't give them up. Miraculously, I had a three-day layover in Seoul the next month, so I signed up for the tour. I had to dress up, and I had to wear sleeves and a badge, but I didn't have a jacket, so I wore a blouse over a dress.

It was scary, because North Koreans take their communism very seriously, as Otto Warmbier would tell you if he were still alive today. The war room had a red line down the middle, and we could walk around the table into North Korea. The North Korean soldiers were facially impassive—they looked through you as if you were garbage—inconsequential, and not even a person. And their guns were loaded. The South Koreans in the war room were noticeably friendlier, albeit with the same ammunition. It was an air that was hard to understand or even conceive of in this day and age when we finally seemed to be coming together as a world. Of course, this was before 9/11 and the current racial and religious tensions.

Outside, in the demilitarized zone, all we could see was jungle and a town. North Korea had a fake village set up with loud speakers blaring, proclaiming how wonderful life was in the north compared to the south, our tour guide said when we asked him to interpret. The North Koreans planned to tunnel through the thirteen miles of rock between North and South Korea and pop up in downtown Seoul. Our guide said they would be picked off like rats as they tried to come up through the manhole covers. But a military friend of mine says some of the tunnels are wide enough for 100,000 troops and tanks.

We left the war room and were escorted into the tunnels. It was eerie. We hunched over, trying not to scrape our backs and heads in the tight, claustrophobic tunnels of solid rock. There were breathing holes drilled in places, up to the surface, but it was still hot and stifling. The South Koreans are always finding new tunnels, and they light fires in them so the smoke comes out of the air holes. Smoke plumes rise in the foliage, showing how the tunnels snake and branch through the jungle. It was a very weird day… a glimpse into the minds of men that didn't really make sense in today's world.

Korea had seemed like a strange, overpopulated, polluted country before the previous month and this visit. I had toured the land outside the city and learned about their lives. I came away with a better understanding of this part of Asia, and a respect for their culture and their people. I had friends here, and I liked and cared about them. It made the world smaller for me. From then on, I could not pretend otherwise when I watched the evening news back home in Oregon.

Communism is serious business.

LOUSE AND DE LAOS, 2017

There are only five communist countries left in the world. Laos is one of them, and the other four are China, Cuba, North Korea, and Vietnam. I had only been to China and North Korea.

"You're going where?"

"Laos." And so it began:

"Why would anyone want to go to Louse?" "Where is it?" "Be careful." "Don't get sick." "I'm worried about you coming home alive." "Is Kevin going?"

Of course, Kevin *wasn't* going and, of course, I *would* be careful.

I stopped explaining and started planning. The Buddhist New Year celebration is in Luang Prabang, a city in northern Laos. My Laotian girlfriend, Nok, had invited me to go with her years ago. Circumstances had prevented us from going then, so why not now?

I would take Delta to Narita, Japan. ANA and Thai both go to Bangkok, and ANA, Laos Air, and Thai go on to Vientiane, Laos. Of course, this was all contingent on there being seats, because I was going standby.

My friends think I must be great at packing. In truth, I just throw everything, including the kitchen sink, into my large suitcase and plan on using my credit card for anything I forget. I'm not a discount traveler—if I can't afford the trip, I don't go. My packing habits were quickly derailed when I learned there wasn't time to clear customs and recheck my luggage in Japan. I would have to take everything as carry-on luggage or spend the night in Narita. I would need to use my small suitcase and all my liquids would have to fit into a quart-sized bag. *What could I do without?*

Laotian electricity is 230 volts and 50 watts. I have burned up too many "compatible" appliances in my lifetime. I could do without my hair dryer and my flat iron. Besides, Nok must have a hair dryer for her long, jet-black hair. I could buy generic body lotion and other necessities in the Portland airport after security, but my hair and face products were important to me. Without all my normal liquids, I would have more room in my suitcase. Besides, all I needed were summer clothes. Temperatures would be in the high nineties.

"Bring long dresses for the temples," Nok told me. "You have to cover up for the monks. Oh, and my mom lives there now that my dad passed away so we will be visiting her, too. She's a white monk."

I didn't own any temple dresses. *A what? A white monk?* This is why I wanted to go. There is so much I don't know about this world!

"Don't forget your passport picture for the visa," her husband Mike, a former Delta pilot, told me with less than a week to go.

Nowhere had I seen the visa information mentioned.

"Don't worry. I've forgotten mine before and they just charge a little extra and copy your passport photo," Mike said.

"What about our tickets home?" I asked.

"We'll get them from a friend of ours who is a travel agent in Bangkok. Don't worry, we aren't going to leave you alone in a communist country."

Now that's a relief. Wait, Laos is communist?

"Take water decontamination tablets," said my R.N. girlfriend.

I bought a special water bottle and iodine pills and grapefruit extract. *Another liquid for my quart-sized bag. Great.*

Looking at the loads for the flights I wanted to take, I was getting nervous. Should I leave Monday if I couldn't get business class on Sunday? Would my friends' plans be ruined if I were late? They had left the week before and were already there. I talked myself into relaxing. What fun is a vacation if you are stressed out? Then again, I never thought of this trip as a vacation. It would be an education.

Laos is landlocked, so I wouldn't be spentding time at a beach. I wasn't even taking a bathing suit. Nok had a hotel booked in Luang Prabang for $35 a night, and there wasn't a pool. I just hoped they had air conditioning. "I don't want to spend a $100 a night for a hotel," she said. "That's just too much."

My husband rolled his eyes. "You need to tell her you don't want cheap." I hadn't told her I'm a princess when I travel... I had already decided this wasn't my call. Nok used to be a travel agent, and she knows what is an acceptable hotel and what isn't. "I trust her," I told him.

"I'm sure glad I'm not going," he said. So was I. My husband is not an adventurous traveler, and this was going to be an adventure. I opened a book on my shelf called, *One Thousand Places To See Before You Die*. Luang Prabang was one of the thousand. I pulled out another book of my daughter's: *501 Must-visit Destinations*. Everywhere we were going was in the book: Vientiane, Plain of Jars, and Luang Prabang—the best preserved city in southeast Asia! Now I was getting excited.

I decided to leave on the Sunday flight. Walking to my gate at the airport, I wondered if I would even get on. I was number twenty-two out of twenty-eight nonrevenue passengers. The next day looked just as bad. Since all the travel sites like Cheapo Air, Expedia, and Hotwire started selling online tickets, it's much harder to go standby as an airline employee. The good news was that it would only cost me $46 in taxes if I got on.

I was nicely dressed, a stipulation of my nearly-free travel, and I approached the gate agent to ask how it looked. "Oh, you'll get on, you're number eleven out of twelve seats." *How did I move up to eleven? There were that many no-shows?* "But it looks like you'll be in coach," she continued. *Crap. Should I wait until tomorrow?* Eleven hours is a long time in coach, especially with two more flights after Narita.

I waited patiently, plotting my journey from Narita to Bangkok. The standby flight on ANA that I had purchased for $82 had a smiley face emoji, meaning I would probably get on. The next leg to Vientiane, Laos had a noncommittal emoji face instead of the number of seats. At least it wasn't a sad face. *What to do?* I decided to take a full fare flight out of Bangkok to Vientiane. I bought a $100 ticket on Thai. *And quickly realized the Thai flight was out of Don Mueang, another airport in Bangkok over an hour and a half away!* I'm always doing crap like this… getting in a hurry and screwing up. I emailed to cancel it, but my flight was boarding. I would take my chances going standby and eat the $100 I had just wasted. The agent called my name. "We had a business passenger cancel," she said. "Your seat is 1A." I *skipped* down the jet bridge and onto the plane!

After takeoff, lying down in my bed with a comforter and comfortable pillow, I snuggled in. I watched two great movies, *Money Monster* and *Allied*, and ate a delicious dinner. Then I slept until we were descending into Japan. Narita was the hub of my wheel, and I had "spoked" out of here for years. It was like a second home, and it had been twelve years since my last trip. *Why have I waited so long to come back?* Honestly, Fukushima had me spooked about going here, and the North Korea situation wasn't great, either. Dragging my bags through the terminal, I looked out the windows at my former haunt with longing. Akiko lived in Narita, and I would visit her on my way home.

I had to go through security again. They took the expensive body cream I had just bought in the Portland Airport after clearing security there. It wasn't much to lose when my business class seat would have cost me $8000 if I had paid full fare.

The next leg on ANA wasn't so great, but I got on. As an "offline" standby we are only allowed to go coach. I was in an exit row, so I could put my foot up on the door slide, but it was also near the bathroom and galley. Despite my great sleep on the way to Narita, it was nighttime at home. My mood became darker and darker as the hours ticked by. I was dying when we reached Bangkok. Exhausted and grumpy, I decided not to leave the airport. There was a hotel on the top floor, and even though it was expensive, it was easy, quiet, and included a shower and breakfast. Little did I know that it was my last warm shower for a week. I slept the sleep of the dead.

The next morning I checked into Bangkok Airways. Despite the noncommittal emoji face, I got on standby, with plenty of room! A 'neutral face' is all they ever show to non-revenue passengers, unless it is a full flight, and then it is a sad face. I had a second free breakfast in their amazing lounge, and then boarded. I was in the last row, but it was a short flight. The city of Bangkok gave way to rice fields as we flew north. I had always wanted to see more of Thailand, and this was my chance. Laos is just across the Mekong River, and the two cultures are joined in history.

When we landed in Vientiane I could barely control myself... I was here! I was the last one off the plane, but surely most of the passengers were Laotian. Customs should be a breeze. Then I saw the visa line.

There were over thirty people waiting. An Australian lady was in front of me, and a mother and her beautiful daughter, from the UK, were behind us. We all realized we didn't have the forms we needed, and took turns holding each other's place in line as we went to get them. The mother didn't know you needed money and a passport photo, so she went to the cash machine while every single guy in line hit on her daughter. It was funny, and fun, and even though we were in line for an hour, the time passed fast. Nok and Mike were waiting for me outside.

I felt wonderful. I had slept five hours on the flight over, six hours in the hotel, and I had eaten two breakfasts. Nok drove, because she claimed Mike was much too aggressive a driver for Laos, and she was afraid he would end up in jail. Laos doesn't take their communism as seriously as North Korea, but that doesn't mean you should do anything stupid. We found a little restaurant, and Mike ordered a banana shake. That sounded good to me, but Nok said no. Mike could eat anything, but Mike's mom ended up in the hospital on an IV a few years back with uncontrollable diarrhea when she visited, and Nok didn't like the shape of the ice cubes. Good to know. I ordered a Beerlao.

Nok suggested that Mike and I get a massage while she had her hair done and ran some errands. We quickly agreed. In hindsight, that should have been my clue that my hair would look like crap the entire time I was in Laos. *Why would she get her hair washed and dried?*

Bamboo bridge in Luang Prabang

Walking around the Plain of Jars site 2 with my girlfriends

Buddhist temple cave in Laos

Cows in the street of a Laotian village after a monsoon rain

I wasn't in Kansas anymore, not that it looked anything like Kansas. The gilded temple across the street was plated in real gold. Another notable, non-Kansas-like difference was the electrical wiring going every which way, with tangles on every street corner. This was definitely a third world country, where the typical Laotian lived on $1.25 a day.

The massage felt heavenly, and two hours under a fan went by way too fast. We drank our delicious bael stone apple tea, paid our $15 apiece, and followed Nok back to the van. This time our destination was the Mekong River. Nok pointed out some million-dollar homes that had been built recently, along with a hotel complex where nests of cobras were found when it was built. Land near the river was never premium in Vientiane, so it was wild and undeveloped until now. Nok's dad had been dumbfounded when he learned that land in the country or near water in the United States was more expensive and desirable than being in the city.

There was an impromptu market set up, so we paid the entrepreneur who guided us into the parking spot three thousand kip: about thirty-six cents. We passed vendors selling snacks, fish, fruits and vegetables, quail eggs, and cooked Lao food that was foreign to me. "You don't want to eat any of this," Nok informed me—as if I were tempted.

She pointed at the statue in the distance that we were walking to. "That's Chao Anouvong, our last king in 1828." There was a shrine around the statue, and Nok read the Thai words in English. The sun was setting across the river on the Thailand shore of the Mekong. Families were playing and listening to music in the nearby park, and Laos' "White House" was in the distance. I almost pinched myself because the scene was so surreal. I couldn't believe I made it to Laos without a hitch.

We spent five days in Vientiane. I met Nok's friends and family, and learned new things every day about the culture and history of Laos. When I flew into Bangkok years ago, I didn't learn that much about the culture or day-to-day life. Don't get me wrong;

I learned a lot, but nothing like this experience. Nok took us to a funeral dinner for a friend's mom, where I tried Lao food and drink that was safe, and to the shrine upstairs. I went to several local restaurants with her friends and learned I cannot keep up with Lao drinking… every two seconds someone is toasting and you are supposed to drink. It reminded me of playing the drinking game 'Quarters,' which I always lost. Or the German celebration of Octoberfest. Hoy, hoy, hoy!

I lost count of how many temples we visited. Monks are not allowed to touch women, and the rules about covering yourself are to protect their efforts at celibacy. It was a hundred degrees outside on the days I wore my long dresses. I felt like I was melting half the time and kept checking the ground for puddles when not a breath of wind disturbed the hot, humid air.

I've always enjoyed talking to monks in Bangkok and Singapore, and Laos was no different. They are eager to learn and practice their English. I wished I had learned more Lao! I met Nok's mom and her friends, and she called me her "other daughter."

We said goodbye and headed to the airport. There were six of us flying to Phonsavan, including a friend of Nok's, and Jim (another Delta pilot) and his wife, Keak. Jim had helped me years before when Northwest Airlines had tried to fire me for turning down an airplane that wasn't safe to fly, so I was already indebted to him. Keak is Thai, and within seconds I knew why he had married her. She's a sweetheart, and being with her and Nok made the next week even better.

Nok's friend Phoon met us and escorted us to the first class lounge. He is the head of airport security for the country, and he upgraded us to first class. We couldn't believe our good fortune.

Phonsavan is near our next destination, the Plain of Jars. The largest jar on the plain weighs six tons! No one knows when the jars were made because you can't date stone, but best guesses put them at 2000 years old. No one knows what they were for, either, and guesses include burials or water collection. There is no remnant of anything that would yield a clue. The locals think the jars were for rice wine to celebrate a victory over a cruel chieftain. I thought I would get tired of looking at jars for hours, but it was fascinating. They are all different shapes and sizes. Many of them are broken into pieces from the bombs that landed nearby.

There are so many unexploded bombs around this part of Laos that only a few sites have been cleared. We only went to sites one and two, but there are three. Mike explained how cluster bombs worked as we walked around, and why the small ones were so effective and still dangerous. We had already seen a collection of bombs when we registered in Phonsavan as tourists, and it was sobering. (No one can travel without registering in each locale.)

Three hundred adults and children are still killed or maimed each year in Laos, by unearthing unexploded ordances. Mike said that if he had been one of the pilots who dropped the bombs in the Vietnam War he would not be allowed in Laos, even as Nok's husband.

WE HAVE THIS hotel to ourselves and it is crazy-fun to be the only patrons, high above the city of Phonsavan. Last night, we had a big dinner in the large dining room with food Nok ordered from town. The rice and stir-fry were excellent. The meat was a little tough, but with a good flavor. Some of it is more like jerky, and you can pick it up with your fingers. The fish soup was spicy, and just okay. *I can't quell my excitement, and I don't try.* We all goof around, posing on the deck after dinner and watching the moon rise.

The next morning I sat outside in my pajamas. The temperature is perfect, as I drink my '3 in 1' instant coffee on my deck. I'm listening to roosters crow and dogs bark. There's a chickadee in the pine tree, and a butterfly flitting about. It's smoggy as can be. I'm watching the red sun rise, literally and figuratively.

A very loud communist announcement begins, and is blasted all over the town. I can't understand a word of it. Laos is even more of the experience I expected it to be.

Our driver never told us how bad the road was or how long a drive it is to the hot springs, unless he told Nok in Laotian. We had a great lunch on the way, with a crazy rainstorm that went through and deluged the town. The cows walked through the muddy street, and we bought bamboo, watermelon, and noodles alongside the road to eat later. The scenery was so fascinating that we weren't even *that* disappointed when we arrived at the hot springs. *Well, maybe a little.* They weren't pretty, just hot! We hiked to a pond, walked around it, felt the water, and walked back. The rooms were tiny, with a bathtub filled from the springs. At least there were some concrete pools outside, but no one was using them. Nok still wanted to experience the place, so we had a beer as they filled a pool for us. She showed me how to don a Lao bathing suit—just a piece of material she wrapped around me and tied. It was a blast, and it was her birthday, so we laughed and talked until we were too hot to stay in the water any longer. We dried off and headed for our hotel.

I shared a hotel room with one of Nok's friends. She watched *Thailand's Got Talent* on television. I couldn't understand a word, but the judge's inflections were just like our American judges! Another show was called the *Hidden Voice,* and you had to figure out which person was singing. We were both laughing, trying to guess who was lip-syncing and who wasn't.

The next day my roommate headed back to Vientiane, while the rest of us piled into our van on the way to Luang Prabang. The road was winding and dangerous, with ninety-degree turns and hairpin curves. We knew it was at least a six-hour drive, and Nok told our driver to go slow and make it an eight-hour one. It didn't matter how long it took us as long as we made it, we had decided. The highway winds through village after village, and each one is different. There were moms with babies in slings, children bathing in waterfalls, people sitting in the doorways because their homes were too hot, goats and chickens, landslides, slash burns, terraced fields, and steep drop-offs. School children were walking home midday, some in their uniforms. Nok said they get a two- or three-hour lunch, or at least she had as a child.

We had lunch at a restaurant with a great view. I was eating delicious Lao chips that Jim and Keak had bought. Nok said they were mushrooms and that she ate a whole bag of them one time and got really dizzy. *Say what?* I slowed down on the mushroom chips. The meat tasted funny to me, but Nok said it wasn't bad and wouldn't make we sick. On the way out, there were some antlers on a cutting table, so we think I was eating venison. I'll never know for sure, but I didn't get sick. We were all drinking a lot of water in the heat, and being careful.

The winding road took forever, and the driver said there were rebels in the hills, and that some of the towns were not friendly. In fact, there were hidden airbases near some of the towns, and lots of secrets still kept. Nok sat up front through some of the riskier towns, and I ducked down in others. Big trucks thundered by, and came within inches of the kids playing close to the highway. They passed us on hairpin curves with no guard rail and no where to go. When we reached Luang Prabang we all breathed a sigh of relief.

As we neared the city, the Buddhist New Year celebration was in full swing. Everyone threw water at us. We checked into our guesthouse, and I was thrilled with my thirty-five-dollar room. Just lying on the bed for an hour made all the difference in the world. Now I was ready to explore!

We walked up to the main street, looking for a dinner restaurant. We ran into friends of Nok's on the main street. She grew up here, and in Vientiane, so she knows everyone. It was fun to feel safe, and the streets weren't that crowded, except during parades.

Temples and monks, French architecture everywhere, and rivers on both sides of Luang Prabang meant that there was always something to see. We had massages during the hottest parts of the day, or read in our rooms.

One night we went to a house blessing at Nok's aunt's house, paired with a birthday party for her five-year-old niece. We were welcomed by Nok's young cousin who spoke French, Lao, and English. She gave us bottles of water, and I couldn't believe how good her English was. We sat on the couch waiting for the ceremony, baking in the heat. They needed nine monks for the blessing, and apparently some were stuck in the New Year's traffic. When at last all the monks were there, the fans were turned off so they could light the candles.

If I thought it was hot before, I was wrong. The ceremony was over an hour long, and the chanting and singing went on forever. Mike, Jim, and I thought we might pass out in the sweltering heat, but Nok, Keak, and the other locals seemed not to notice. Afterwards, outside with a Heineken, I started to feel better. My tablemates were Vietnamese children, and again, they spoke very good English. I so enjoyed talking to them, and I was glad I had come.

Another day, we joined Nok's friends on the side of the road throwing water at passersby. Everyone was soaking wet, and we were all cracking up. The temperature was probably a hundred degrees, but we were comfortable as long as we were doused with water. Drinking beer and laughing, it was an incredible afternoon.

I wasn't "allowed" to have the fruit drinks or coconut juice unless Nok looked at the ice cubes, the knives, and cutting surface. (Thank goodness she was so proactive. Our last night in Laos I had fruit shakes and was sick, but it didn't last long and that was the only time.)

Nok rented another van and driver for the day, and there were eight of us now. We stopped at an elephant preserve first. The elephants were rescued from lumber operations, and are treated like kings and queens now. It was too windy to ride them, because they get unpredictable on windy or stormy days, the handlers said. I had ridden an elephant before, so I just wanted to feed them and touch them! The elephants all liked bananas better than the bamboo, so I bought the rest of the bananas and we took turns feeding them. We were all laughing and having the best time with the baby. What a cutup! He would reach behind my back for a banana, but by then it was in my other hand. He was clever, and talented, performing tricks as we clapped. A few hours later, it was time to go. I hated to leave, but the waterfall was next.

Seeing pictures of the Kuang Si waterfall is nothing like being there. Glacial lakes in North America are the only bluish-green color I can compare the water to. Think Yellowstone, but cool not hot. It was simply breathtaking. As we walked along the path, we reached one waterfall after another, each more lovely than the one before. Looking up at the last waterfall, the largest and best of the dozen or so, I was glad I wasn't climbing it in my slippery sandals.

I was wrong. I tried to beg off, but followed them nonetheless. I slipped halfway up, and clunked my camera on a rock. Nok's friend Tony carried my camera after that, and I made it to the top. There wasn't much of a view, but it was like being in a jungle-park. There was a rope swing, a boat, picnic tables, and bottled water. We could see the guesthouse across the valley where we were going to have lunch. I didn't want to leave here, either. At last we headed down.

The waterfall at the guesthouse was as elegant as the one we hiked to. Lunch was outside on the water. Little kids were swimming without suits, chasing each other and giggling as they jumped off the falls. There was jerky, bamboo, steamed rice, and all sorts of Lao dishes. My favorite was the blackened chicken, seasoned with lemongrass. And dark Beerlao. The teak and rosewood buildings surrounding us were beautiful, with carved elephants and stunning gardens. And then the best part... swimming in the waterfall at the guesthouse in our Lao bathing suits. I even dove off the top without losing my suit!

It's almost time to go home. Keak, Jim, and I rent a longboat for the afternoon of our last day. Our longboat is extremely stable, but Nok won't come. She can't swim.

Our destination is the Pak Ou caves, two or three hours upstream from Luang Prabang on the Mekong River. Keak says the caves were once a famous king's place of worship, but then he gave them to the people. Some people call Buddhist caves *cave temples*, and this one was filled with thousands of Buddha images.

We pass by water buffalo, goats, elephants, and cows. Some of the homes are spectacular, especially in a country this poor. People are swimming, picnicking, and fishing on the banks. We pass monks in a boat, and Keak says they are lucky monks... in Thailand monks can't even drive a car. We pass an elephant preserve, restaurants, houseboat communities, and villages known for their silk. It is the best way to end our trip, leaning back and relaxing on the cool of the river. We end the day on a restaurant overlooking the river, and finally celebrate Nok's birthday with candles and singing. The next day we are back at the airport with Nok's good friend Phoon, in the first class lounge.

LAOS WAS MORE of an education than a vacation. It's silly how happy I am to be home, and how happy I was when I was there. In Laos, lying in bed, I heard roosters, loud propaganda speakers, motorbikes, and people partying. Here, at home, all I hear are birds and wind. I think about Laotians out farming their fields. I'm surrounded by fields, too. I can't imagine finding bombs here.

***I wish our country had never dropped
all those bombs.***

CORREGIDOR AND WORLD WAR II

Flying over Midway Island in the Pacific Ocean, seeing Suicide Cliff in Saipan, and listening to pilots who were history buffs, I became more and more interested in World War II. The next time I had a long layover in Manila, the captain told me I should go to Corregidor, a tadpole shaped island in Manila Bay. It wasn't a hard sell. I love boat rides, and it was a beautiful day. Steve, the flight engineer, came with me. We joked about our boat, the Ho Ho, being Slow Slow. It took us six hours, round trip, to go sixty-two miles, but it was worth every minute.

Corregidor is a memorial to the soldiers who lost their lives in the Pacific in World War II. The island is a marvel. We pulled into the dock and stepped onto an island frozen in time, surrounded by ruins and guns. There is a hotel, a restaurant, and a pool. It would be incredible to spend the night and explore the entire island on the hotel bicycles.

Corregidor was fortified before World War I with fixed gun batteries. The tunnel system underneath Malinta Hill was built during World War II. General MacArthur's headquarters were inside Malinta Tunnel, along with barracks, a *thousand*-bed hospital, stores, shops, and storage rooms. It was imperative for the Japanese to take Corregidor to get to Manila and take the Philippines. Without the use of the Manila Harbor the Japanese would have been severely handicapped. Bataan, of Bataan Death March fame, fell in April 1942. Corregidor fell to the Japanese in May 1942. Manila remained in Japanese hands until the end of the war.

The tunnel system under Corregidor goes on for miles. Standing under solid rock, we learned the history of the fortress as gunfire, explosions, and lighting effects went off around us. We felt like we were revisiting 1942. Being underground in the hospital where tuberculosis was once rampant was so realistic that we got the willies standing there. It was like being in a movie, and I've never forgotten the experience or what I learned down there.

Steve and I breathed a sigh of relief to be back in the sunlight after our tour. We took gulps of the fresh air and realized we had been holding our breath. The captain was right. It was an incredible experience. I wish we could teach history as effectively in our schools as it was taught to us that day.

Traveling is the best way to learn.

AMSTER, AMSTER, DAM, DAM, DAMN!

A girlfriend of mine worked for our airline's radio department. Whenever I had long layovers that corresponded to her days off, she would use her travel privileges to come with me. She met me in San Francisco, Boston, London, Amsterdam, Manila, Narita, and Bangkok. We had adventures all over the world, but our funniest was our trip to Amsterdam.

We decided to take the wine and cheese tour through the canals. As luck would have it, we had a new, inexperienced boat captain who happened to be a woman. The captain hit the side of every bridge we went under! We were sitting at the back of the boat by ourselves, at a table. Every time the boat hit the concrete wall of a bridge, wine glasses would tumble off the shelf behind us and shatter to smithereens. The passengers would turn around and give us dirty looks, like it was somehow our fault. We started giggling, then ended up laughing so hard that we couldn't stop.

When the weather was good, I loved taking the train to cheese towns like Edam and Gouda, just to walk along the canals and see the windmills. It was like stepping back in time, with the cows and sheep munching grass as the blades turned slowly in the wind. The villages were fun to explore, and I loved sitting outside drinking wheat beer and eating bread and cheese.

I didn't always leave Amsterdam. Sometimes we would make a plan for dinner, and afterwards, when we walked the Red Light District, the pilots educated me on the shops and oddities you could buy there. One shop had 148 different blowup dolls, with different hair colors and styles and professions. Pot smoking was, of course, legal, and pipes and pot were everywhere. We found ourselves holding our breath so as not to flunk the drug test the next day!

THE PARENTS OF Portland, Oregon started a program called "Bring History Alive" in our public schools. Volunteer parents would study a character out of history, dress up in costume, and do a presentation for the students. It was a big hit. The first grade teacher at our grade school decided we should try it, too. Unfortunately, I was the only volunteer. I studied the lives of famous people like Martin Luther King, Cleopatra, and Mark Twain while I was on my trips. The positive response from the students made it worth the effort.

The history teacher at the high school wanted me to be Anne Frank. I memorized everything I could about her life, her diary, and the Holocaust. I had wanted to see the Anne Frank House, but I was always too tired to wait in line. Now I had a purpose. I bid a trip to Amsterdam and waited in the rain for hours. Once I got inside, I was surprised at how small the house was. It was *tiny*. I tried not to cry, walking through the rooms where Anne and her family once lived, imagining what it was like for them.

The teacher planned my talk to coincide with Anne's birthday. I dyed my hair and put on a frumpy, nondescript outfit. I made my face as pale as Anne's must have been after hiding in the house for two years, and put dark circles under my eyes.

The kids were boisterous teenagers, but they were silent as I told them about "my" life. They asked questions, and at the end of the hour the teacher brought out a cake with fifteen candles on it with "Happy Birthday Anne" written out of frosting. As I cut the cake, I told them it was my last birthday, coincidentally the same age as most of them.

The two-hour wait in the rain was worth it. The kids had tears in their eyes as they took their pieces of cake from me. I hadn't loaded them into my 747 to fly them to the Anne Frank House, but history came alive for them that day.

Stay open to possibilities. Don't limit yourself.

Shuttered buildings in old Singapore

Cirque du Soleil out my window on Hong Kong Island

FOOT WHAT?

I wanted to explore Singapore, but all I was capable of doing was sleeping by the pool. A week previous I had a bad case of food poisoning and I couldn't quite shake it. Every time I ate anything I remembered why I shouldn't eat at all. The captain was determined to cure me.

"Foot reflexology. It's what you need. It will make you feel better," he informed me. "All the nerves in your body terminate in your feet. A good reflexologist can tell exactly where you are ailing, press on that spot, and stimulate your body to cure itself."

I'd heard about Asian reflexologists. A pilot I knew went to a reflexologist in Manila. He said it hurt like hell, and threatened the reflexologist with a well-placed kick if he did not stop.

"No thanks, I'm not into pain."

"What exactly would you call what you are in now?" he asked.

I wanted to wipe that smug look off his face. "Discomfort. Extreme discomfort. There's a difference."

"It's like a foot massage. I get them all the time, to stay healthy."

"It will hurt. Especially since I'm already sick."

"It only hurts when they hit a spot that is weak in your body. You wince and they proceed more gently."

Wince. I knew it. The other pilot said it hurt worse than knee surgery. And my husband says knee surgery is worse than child-birth, according to a lady he met during recovery. Although I don't believe my husband—I had a thirty-two hour labor with my first child—I get the point. "No thanks. I'll spend the day at the pool relaxing."

But Jerry wouldn't take no for an answer. "It will only take an hour or two out of your day. Come on. What have you got to lose?"

I could lose whatever ground I'd gained the last few days. But I nodded. I'd try anything to feel better than I did.

I DRESS AND meet him in the lobby. We cross the street and go downstairs into the dark bowels of Singapore to the subway. Fifteen minutes later we emerge near the Far East Plaza. The bright daylight is blinding as we walk into a modern shopping area. We weave our way through the maze of chandeliers and marble, upstairs to an area of low ceilings and poor lighting. Singapore is a study in contrasts... new and old, modern and ancient, clean and filthy.

He introduces me to his reflexologist, who takes me into a small room and has me lie down on a table. She washes my feet in warm water laced with peppermint oil and dries them. "Relax," she says, pushing on my foot. "Does any part of your body hurt?"

I shake my head. "Not really," I lie. Just a sore throat, the vestiges of an intestinal flu or food poisoning, and a sore left shoulder and neck. I am treating this like a session with a fortuneteller... I know what hurts and I'm not going to tell.

She hits a spot on my toe that sends me to the roof. I nearly leap off the table, crying out in pain!

"Throat," she says with certainty.

Now I'm really tense. Still, one out of three... Then she pulls out a stick. I grit my teeth. Pressing on the center of my foot, she glances up at me. I push into it. Yes, it hurts, but it's more like deep massage.

"Intestines."

Slowly I start to relax. Or go numb... The rest is not so bad. Except for the ankles and side of my right foot, nothing else makes me cry out at least. I feel a bit nauseous, from all the toxins being released into my bloodstream, my reflexologist says.

"Normal," she assures me. "This is the ovary and this is the sciatic nerve." She powders my foot and wraps it tightly before starting on the other one. She finds a tender spot on my other foot. "Bladder. You need to drink more water."

I nod, gulping. The bladder spot really hurts. That and another spot for my throat. She works her way up my calf.

"You are really healthy. Very good. Do you eat much red meat?"

I shake my head. I try to eat fish, chicken, and salads.

"You have too much cholesterol." She says she can feel the lumps in my heels.

Okay, so maybe I do eat more red meat than I should... bacon, steak, ground beef. She finds one more excruciating spot near my left big toe. "Ow!" I shriek.

"Neck," she announces.

Bingo. I am truly amazed that she can feel all that in my foot. Either that or she really is psychic. Now both feet are wrapped in swaddling cloth. She massages my hands, neck, and shoulders. It costs only fifteen American dollars for forty minutes. And it felt good, overall, except for a few spots. I want more!

"Next week, you come back." She hands me a cup of tea.

Jerry, drinking his own tea after a session with a different reflexologist, says, "See? Was it so bad?"

I shake my head. Some of my skepticism is gone. I need to be more open-minded. He says I should have reflexology done regularly. Not every day, mind you, but as often as possible. I go back to my hotel, expecting my feet to ache. *They don't.* I notice my urine smells extremely strong. I drink lots of water and tea for the rest of the day, to flush my system. And I feel better.

The next day I notice I am getting a vaginal discharge. *Great.* So much for reflexology. I didn't want to get sick; I wanted to get better. Every symptom I have goes away in a few days. I buy a book on reflexology in Hong Kong that explains the strong smell and discharge are normal after reflexology... your body is cleansing itself, the author explains. I'm still skeptical, but the whole experience was good. I become a regular, often getting three or four treatments on one layover! I play scientist, noticing that sometimes the practitioners are good, other times they don't really have the knack. But I always feel better afterwards.

ONE OF THE times I took a girlfriend with me, I became a true believer. It was her first time. The Chinese man working on her was very perplexed when he came to one spot on her foot. He said he felt nothing, and was worried. She asked what part of the body the spot was for, and he searched for the word, finally answering, "Baby."

"Oh," she said. "I've had a hysterectomy."

The man was perplexed. As she explained, his face lit up. It made sense to him. The nerves went nowhere, so he felt nothing.

WE PILOTS ARE not known for our open-mindedness. We are linear, logical thinkers. After years of flying the Pacific Rim, I am no longer close-minded. Acupuncture, muscle kinesiology, and healing herbs no longer seem farfetched. I bid Singapore and Hong Kong lay-overs for reflexology as often as possible, since they are the best I've found. There is a place in Hong Kong that is my favorite, and it is called "The Big Bucket." They roll in a "big bucket" or cask, and you put your feet in it. There seem to be golf balls under the liner on the bottom, and the fragrant water gels around your feet, tingling and cleansing them before the reflexology.

I'm a believer.

SINGAPORE

Singapore was my favorite layover city. Most of the pilots hated the heat and humidity there, but growing up in Florida, I could handle this hot, humid paradise near the equator. My only problem was deciding what to do there. The guys would laugh at my exuberance, but there was always something new to see!

I visited the Jurong Bird Park often, and one of the trainers let me go behind the scenes with him to help care for the birds. The Crocodile Farm was next door, but it was smelly and a little freaky, as the entertainers would put their heads in the crocodile's mouths! I'm not into witnessing death or injury, so I only went there once.

The Singapore Zoo was the best. Singapore is a rainforest, and the zoo is set up so that you are almost always walking next to the water. Tropical birds and tamarin monkeys filled the trees, beautiful heliconia and ginger plants lined the paths, and you could walk through the kangaroo enclosure. Komodo dragons—huge carnivorous lizards—were a novelty to me, and I knew their habitat was in nearby Indonesia. I loved being up close and personal with chimpanzees, orangutans, and elephants. The zoo is open nights, too, with hyena feeding frenzies and eerie night noises. One of the employees admitted they kill poisonous snakes all the time, so I stayed on the path and watched my step!

I enjoyed getting to know the real Singapore. When I first started flying there, the old city was intact. But a huge renewal effort was going on, and Singaporeans were being moved farther and farther out of the city into giant, high-rise apartment buildings. Soon Singapore was losing its old world charm, with modern skyscrapers going up everywhere. It was almost too late when the government realized tourists loved the old-style buildings and atmosphere.

Chinatown, Arab Street, and Little India were always fun. There were gardens and neighborhoods to explore, and interesting foods to sample. One layover, I was flying with another woman pilot who signed us up for a cooking class at Sunrice Academy in Fort Canning Park. First, we toured the spice garden, and then we went to the kitchen classroom. We prepared our lunch with spices from the garden that we ground using a mortar and pestle. Watching the chef in the overhead mrror, we prepared and cooked all our courses. The smells were heavenly. We dished everything up and ate on the deck. Everything was delicious, which was shocking since both of us are good pilots but not great cooks!

Sentosa Island is mostly for tourists, but we golfed there on my first layover. Monkeys chattering in the trees, cockatoos flying overhead, and a warning not to retrieve your ball when it went into the rough… there were poisonous snakes! Sitting in the bar at the end of the day, I again had a surreal feeling. *Am I really here?*

Raffles Long Bar was the best place to read on a rainy day. When I wasn't exploring, I swam in our hotel pool, complete with underwater speakers and a swim-up bar.

The first time I went to Singapore we had a four-day layover. I bought a Sunset guide, and I planned it all out, with the help of the two pilots and our lead flight attendant, Kathleen. Buff, our copilot, found a dinner and dance show. To our surprise, the dancers were topless, like a Las Vegas show, but with buxom Australian women onstage. Buff kept apologizing to Kathleen and me. Ralph, our captain, was too busy ogling the women to eat his dinner. We realized there was more to Singapore than met the eyes.

Seeing Changi prison with Bill Fuchs, a pilot friend of mine, was something I will never forget. His dad was in a Russian prison during World War II. Walking through Changi, Bill recounted some of his dad's horrific experiences. Like I said, seeing Asia with historians and people who know made the war much more real to me.

Bill was trying to take a picture of me by the monorail on Sentosa. There was a monkey in the tree, and he wanted her in the picture, too. "Step to your right. Just a little closer…"

The monkey had babies in the tree, and she leapt down to chase me away! I am senior to Bill, and I think he was trying to "gain a seniority number" by having her take me out. If I ever go to Yellowstone National Park with Bill I'll try to get a picture of him with a buffalo.

From my journal:

Singapore. By the pool. Not too hot—very breezy. At my house, we would call it wind. Here, close to the balmy equator, they call it a breeze. I'm in the shade because I don't want to burn again. Last time, the back of my legs were so red I had to stand at my desk all the way back to Narita. The sun isn't out much today, but when it is, it's scorching.

I'm drinking a banana smoothie. Yum. The palms are swaying. It's so cool how the plants grow up the trunks… large elephant ear leaves. I love the patterns on the deck as the sun shines through the leaves. Shadows on the white umbrellas, too. The delicacy of the flower and the veins in the leaves. Reflection and shadow, my personal favorites. So beautiful. The clouds are a gorgeous, puffy white, floating by and disappearing fast. Wispy pieces. Black birds and mynas are flitting about… thieves, stealing food from everyone.

The people in front of me are British and are having tea. Kids are playing in the little pool. Chinese kids with the cutest little suits—old style with one piece tops and blue shorts with lime green trim. I took a few pictures of them sliding down the waterslides.

Strange, on a hot day, to have tea. The lady sunbathing in the very skimpy bikini is German. She just bummed a cigarette off the guy behind her. With a disgusted look, he gave it to her. Maybe a friend, although her husband is waiting? But not as good a friend as she thinks. Her body is beautiful.

This is a five-star hotel, in my world, located on Clark Quay. I'll be surprised if we stay here much longer. It is too nice! There is construction all around, a new subway line going in, and a great location. Chinatown is just three blocks away. I'm walking there this afternoon. Reflexology is only fifteen dollars U.S. for a fifty-minute session that includes the neck and shoulders. I usually walk out of the first place, and then go around the corner and down the hall to another one I like.

There are lots of people here by the pool, but I feel alone. Not lonely, just lazy and relaxed, like I'm on vacation. I am getting comfortable with my abilities as captain. That's a good thing. I saw Bill, the copilot, in the lobby. He looks better. He was positively green yesterday, and on approach and landing he was in the bathroom puking! It was the weirdest feeling being alone up front, with the second officer behind me. Easy, but weird. He says he is feeling a little better, but not great. We have a two-day layover, so he can relax.

I went to Boat Quay for dinner last night, by myself. It is so perfect at night, with all the lights reflecting in the canal, delicious dinner smells, and great music. I think I'll go again tonight. The bouncer took a shine to me, set his drink down on my table, and protected me all night! I continued my education about the Singapore underground, because he told me all kinds of things. I have no idea of the gang structure here, but he is in one, and had a long fingernail on his left hand. Yes, I'm perfectly safe as a tourist, walking around anytime. Do I want to meet him after work? *No!*

Anyway, for Chinese New Year there were lots of colorful chimes, streamers, and lanterns. The restaurant I ate at had white tablecloths, but the napkins were all different colors. The food was so-so. Nasi goreng was the best... rice, shrimp, and chicken fried rice with carrots and peas. I ate the last of it in my room on my balcony! The curry was too hot to eat, or it would have been delicious. The prawn salad was weird... prawns fried in old oil, with mayonnaise on top. The sampans kept going by, with their eyes watching us. I was in bed by nine and slept for ten and a half hours!

Out at the pool, no one comes to take food or drink orders. It amazes me that this nice of a hotel doesn't put more effort into serving people. Labor is cheap, I guess, but they all stand around until you make the effort to walk over to them. Maybe it is the hot sun near the equator that sucks out all the motivation…

People wear bathrobes out to the pool from their rooms, and they look like they are in pajamas. Lots of us beached beluga whales out here today. We are going to burn to a crisp.

I switched rooms to a pool balcony. I love this hotel. It's the third one I've stayed at over the years in Singapore, and they've all been great. But a balcony makes it even better! One more day here. My gosh, the girl who just went into the water was falling out of her top! Maybe she's Australian. What a cute bikini. She's the one drinking tea.

So many memories.

I went to Malaysia on a bus tour to Kukup fishing village and made new friends at lunch.

MALAYSIA

It took me a few years of flying to Singapore before I ventured north to Malaysia. There was so much to see and do in Singapore that I couldn't see any reason to leave. But I did want to see more of Southeast Asia, so I booked a bus trip to Kukup Fishing Village on the Malaysian coast. Guided tours are safe and fun, and I love meeting people and getting off the beaten path.

Our tour group set off early in the morning, and stopped in the capital of Malaysia, Johor Bahru. We saw the Istana Besar, the royal palace of the Sultan of Johor, and tried some street food. Our guide suggested peanut pancakes, and they were delicious—egg whites, peanuts, and sugar! The market reminded me of Bangkok. I also bought salty tapioca chips... they tasted like potato chips. We boarded the bus and our next stop was a rubber plantation.

I had no idea how they harvested the white, sticky fluid. It was fascinating—like being in Vermont and tapping trees for maple syrup! The AIDS virus was in full swing, and the economy of Malaysia benefitted from this deadly disease, as there was a huge need for surgical gloves.

The graveyards we saw along the way were elaborate. Built on hillsides, the ornate sites were tiled and gilded with gold. The Chinese believe that being buried on a hill gets you closer to God, we were told, and they also believed that being buried with all your possessions guaranteed your wealth and position in the next world. However, graverobbers knew the treasures graves held, and the profession was becoming quite lucrative. With the advent of video cameras, the Chinese decided that being buried with a picture of their possessions was just as good. I'm sure the widows were happier too, now that they could keep their deceased husband's worldly goods!

The Malaysian homes had pet monkeys and birds, with bars on the windows. The kids were dressed in pajamas, and they smiled and waved as we drove by.

When we arrived at the fishing village, it was so dilapidated and poor that we were shocked. Our guide told us there was no plumbing, and the toilets were just holes in the floor.

We walked along the boardwalk, peeking in a few homes, since there were no doors. The kids were playing Nintendo Three, a version that wasn't even out in the States! I noticed all the homes had electricity going to them.

It all depends on your priorities, I decided. Who needs window glass and doors when you have video games?

We stopped at a nearby restaurant for lunch, and ate fresh fish and vegetables, before going to see the fish farm. We learned that the sewage from the houses dropped into the water and the tide carried it away. To the fish farm. We looked at each other in horror.

When I returned home, I told my daughter's kindergarten teacher I had been to Malaysia. "Did you go to Kukup? I loved that fishing village. The kids were even playing video games!"

Apparently, I wasn't as far off the beaten path as I had thought.

SNAKES

Growing up in Florida, I got used to snakes. We had three deadly kinds: moccasins, diamondback rattlesnakes, and coral snakes. But none of them compared to the snakes in Singapore.

Some pilots decided to walk from the orchid farm to the Singapore zoo one day. There was a snake hanging from a tree above them, and they stopped to study it. When they reached the zoo they described the snake to one of the workers who spoke English. A look of terror crossed his face. It was a Blue Malaysian Coral Snake, one of the most fatally poisonous snakes in the world.

When my girlfriend and I went to the same zoo one night, we thought about taking the walking tour. But we were both leery after the stories we had heard. So, we asked one of the workers how many snakes they killed during a twenty-four hour period. "Not many during the day, but at least three each night." We took the tram instead.

Sitting on the Singapore River one day, I was under a restaurant tent with the other patrons as the rain poured down. And I do mean poured. It was a full-blown monsoon, and every few minutes the tent roof would get too full and dump a huge amount of water beside us, drenching our feet. We were all laughing, and I was writing postcards, listening to the conversation at the table behind me. Yes, I'm an eavesdropper.

There were two couples, and the women were from Texas. Their husbands were from Australia, and they were all expats living in Singapore. They were so funny that I couldn't keep from laughing.

"I say, let's invent a new game for the tourists," one of the guys said in his heavily accented Aussie voice. "Identify the dead animals floating down the Singapore Drainage Ditch."

Sure enough, a pig floated by, then a bedraggled owl on a log, and even a dead cat. It was disgusting, but they made it funny. I couldn't help but crack up. This followed on the heels of a conversation about face creams and women who pay too much for something that "plumps" your cells.

Suddenly, one of the women leaned forward and tapped me on the shoulder, pointing. "Look at the huge snake!"

"That's not a snake," I laughed. "That's a branch." It was about thirty feet long… too long to be a snake.

"Oh really? When was the last time you saw a branch swim upriver?"

She had a point, and as realization dawned, the "branch" turned and swam towards us! We tipped our chairs over, drenching ourselves as we whacked the tent stake, trying to get away. At the last minute, it turned and swam on, but we were still freaked out by our close call with the giant python. At least it wasn't one of Singapore's poisonous varieties, we reassured each other. Catching our breath, we all ordered more beer, and they invited me to sit with them, since I was listening in already. We had a great time whiling the afternoon away as the rain beat down. My stomach hurt the next day from laughing so long and hard.

You never know what the day will bring.

TYPHOONS AND MONSOONS

I grew up with hurricanes, so I knew the power and havoc crazy weather could wreak. As a little kid in Delaware, there were times when the swings on my swing set went wild, wrapping around the top bar. I remember the aftermath of a winter storm at Rehoboth Beach with the huge Horsey House sitting cockeyed in the sand, and the fronts of hotels sheared off by the waves. You could see inside the hotel rooms, like the back of a dollhouse. The bumper cars we loved to ride were scattered like toys, and the trampolines were ripped from the ground and gone. Dad and Uncle Alden dragged bedsteads and soda fountains out of the ocean the next summer while we kids watched in awe.

Typhoons in Hong Kong and the rest of Asia were fun to watch from the ground only. Thunderstorms were an experience of their own because they grew so fast in the tropics, reaching over 50,000 feet in just a few hours. Flying at night from Japan to Singapore was often exciting. The huge "towering Qs" (cumulus clouds) were a sight to behold from the cockpit, with active bolts of lightning spiking from cloud to cloud, cloud to ground, and even inside the formations. I was awed by the power of nature as we threaded our way through them.

Radar is attenuated by weather, which means it is absorbed. Because the energy is absorbed, you never knew, when you went around a huge cell, whether it would be clear on the other side, or solid thunderstorms. Fuel is always an issue when diverting around weather, as the alternate airports in the South China Sea are few and far between. Flying is serious business.

Hong Kong's old airport, Kai Tak, was situated on a precarious slice of land in Kowloon, and the east end of the runway ended at the South China Sea. The west end was a series of hills topped with skyscrapers. I loved flying into Kai Tak in decent weather. It was a challenge, with a turn at a billboard that was painted like an orange checkerboard. Descending through four hundred feet, turning, with tall buildings on either side was an incredible rush. There was usually a crosswind, and I welcomed a break from the routine—a chance to use my flying skills. But I never flew in or out of Hong Kong during a typhoon, only before or after one hit.

The worst monsoons I experienced were in Hong Kong, Indonesia, and Singapore. Singapore was a rainforest, so I expected it to rain, but the severity was intense, even to a Floridian. Some days I would hole-up in Raffles Bar, reading a book and drinking a Singapore Sling as the rain came down in sheets so blinding you couldn't see through it.

We flew near many active volcanoes in the Pacific Ring of Fire, and of course we avoided them when we could. This is easier said than done. You can see the plumes during the day, but they look like clouds of haze. At night, you hope the plane in front of you reports it because you cannot see the plume on the radar. Radar picks up moisture, not dry ash. If the windshield begins to display a crackled spider web of light, otherwise known as Saint Elmo's fire, and the cockpit smells like sulfur, you turn around immediately. Volcanic ash will melt inside the engines and coke them up so badly that no air can pass through the blades. A British Air flight lost all four engines in 1982 while flying over Indonesia and inadvertently flying through an eruption of Mount Galunggung at night.

The worst wind shear I encountered was at Japan's Narita International "New Tokyo" Airport, located sixty miles to the east of Tokyo, in the middle of miles and miles of rice patties. The runway is long, and approaches are usually stable and predictable, although the gusty crosswinds are always a challenge. One day everyone was diverting to other airports because the shear was so bad. The first approach left us reeling and shaken. The captain wanted to try again, but the flight engineer and I vehemently disagreed. It was unsafe. We wanted to divert to Tokyo's Haneda Airport, where flights were landing safely.

The captain entered holding, ignoring us. He was waiting for conditions to improve. We all want to land at our intended destination, as we are exhausted and tired, but not at the expense of safety. Twenty minutes later, he decided to try again, because there had been no more reports of wind shear! Of course not, we argued, because *no one has tried to land.*

He promised us he would go around immediately and fly to Haneda if the approach was unstable. We believed him. *Suckers.* The approach was as rough as before. We told him to "go around" when we hit a twenty-knot plus shear. He wouldn't. A huge gust of wind caught our 747 and flipped us ninety degrees to the right at only two hundred feet above the ground! I was looking at the ground out my *side* window. I knew my life was over. I was going to die, and I hoped it would be quick.

Miraculously the plane righted itself, and the captain flared and landed. Everyone in the back cheered so loudly we could hear them upstairs and through the door! No other flights landed in Narita that day. We were it. Everyone else diverted. The flight engineer and I were too angry to talk to the captain. We wouldn't go out with him to dinner. The flight engineer told me this was it; he was retiring to live on his boat in Belize. He had had enough of idiot captains trying to kill him.

Believe it or not, we received letters of commendation from the company a few weeks later. What a joke. So much for the crew concept, Cockpit Resource Management, and safety. When you don't follow CRM, that is, using your crewmembers as valuable resources, you are a fool.

I didn't fly with fools often.

Drenched after a monsoon rain on Lantau Island

MACAU

My sixth grade teacher, Mrs. Yates, nourished my appetite for travel. We always read the Scholastic newsletters about the current world politics to augment our history book. When I finished my work early I would read from her collection of giant fairy tale books, never dreaming I would go to such exotic places as Siam, now known as Thailand.

At age thirty-three, my trips to Asia evoked strong emotions in me. I only went to Macau once—out of Hong Kong—before Portugal's lease ran out on July 1, 1997. Jet lag takes its toll on my memory, so this is from my journal:

MACAU: STEVE AND I went to Macau yesterday. Wow! I just couldn't believe I was actually there!

The round trip was only forty dollars U.S. I had been to Batam, Indonesia on a jet boat, but these Turbo Cats, built in Singapore by FBM Mfg., were incomparable. They really get up and move! We zoomed by other boats on the harbor as if they were standing still. I realize that anything would be fast next to the tub we had just taken to Corregidor two days before, but this was like floating on a cushion of air. Every once in a while, going by another boat, I would get an out-of-body sensation of speed and power. When flying the 747, we level out above a solid layer of clouds on descent whenever we can, just to get that feeling of speed.

Sometimes the hovercraft felt like a fast speedboat, but we never slammed onto the water. We passed a beautiful resort with Phuket-style villas, and I memorized its location so I could go back there on vacation. There was a movie on inside the cabin that was only half over as we reached Macau… forty miles in fifty minutes! Steve and I joked that we had only taken out three junks on the way. It was incredible.

Visions of Vasco de Gama danced in my head as I stood on the wall of the Citadel of Sao Paulo de Monté to view Mainland China. I was standing on the wall of the oldest European settlement of the Far East. It was breathtaking.

Macau is such a contrast of old—from 1557—and new—the Guia Circuit Macau Grand Prix, held there every year. The ruins of Saint Paul's church dominate the foreground. The intricate and intriguing, modern architecture of rounded balconies and varied roof styles lie behind the church. Many of the buildings were painted Miami Vice colors, with white shutters and trim accenting the pinks, yellows, blues, and greens.

We met Miyaku, our flight attendant, and her two friends, Hiruma and Shiguru, getting off the boat. They had been in first class on our flight to Hong Kong yesterday. Shiguru's camera was broken, so I took all the pictures as we walked around. They had to leave early, so we had lunch at the Hotel Lisboa after looking at the casino.

My lunch was delicious. I had a Portuguese wine, Caves Sao de Palo '85, caldo verde (green vegetable soup with mashed potato, green vegetables, Portuguese sausage, and olive oil), and Macau crab curry. Miyaku had the "African Chicken," another specialty of Macau that tasted very good. Even Shiguru's codfish or "Bacalhau" was okay. But Steve and Haruma had Tacho—a kind of stew with fat and gizzards and other junk… ugh. None of us were fans of that stew.

After lunch, we said our goodbyes. Steve and I took a cab up to the church on Penha Hill. The view was spectacular and the residences on the way up the hill were amazing. The money… the guards… the expanse. One house, the summer residence of the Bishop of Macau, had an aviary, a pool, a 450SL, and guards and cameras everywhere. It stretched towards the sea, encompassing three city blocks.

We walked down the hill past them all, wondering why so many flags were flying. There seemed to be so much fanfare, and police were everywhere. Intrigued, we found a seat outside a café across from the water and had a few beers. We saw the entourage of the President of Portugal, according to our waiter who had just moved to Macau from Portugal three weeks before. Now we knew why there was so much security around, and we started probing him for more information. I learned more from the waiter than I had learned from Mrs. Yates in all of the sixth grade!

The waiter told us to see the Guia Fortress and lighthouse, the oldest one on the Chinese coast, before going back to Hong Kong. Built in the early 1600s, the Guia Chapel was being renovated and the dust in the air looks like angels and halos. I feel like I am in a fairy tale, on a high that stays with me long after I leave.

Macau. Wow.

How wide is our car?

Colt with Africa and the Straits of Gibralter behind him

SPAIN

When Kevin, Colton, and I decided to go to Spain on vacation in 2004, I was uneasy. There were warnings out for Atlantic air travel after 9/11, and people were edgy about traveling. I wasn't worried about the warnings, but I was worried about vacationing somewhere new, where Northwest Airlines didn't fly. I admit it: I am spoiled. The company arranged our hotels on layovers, and there were always buses or limousines waiting for us outside the airport terminal. Now I had to arrange everything, and it was daunting.

I decided to stay at *paradors* because a captain I flew with told me all about them. Paradors are magnificent old buildings that used to be castles, palaces, convents, monasteries, fortresses, and other historic places transformed into hotels. Spain was under dictatorship until 1975, so it was an enigma to me. I talked to everyone I could, including a friend who had lived there. Our friend thought I had too much driving planned, and not enough down time, so I reconfigured our trip. We decided Andalusia was our priority, and I booked the reservations.

We flew into Madrid and spent the first night in a downtown hotel. There was a fire across the street, so it was an exciting beginning to our vacation. We rode the train to Seville where we saw the tomb of Christopher Columbus. We took a carriage ride and a gypsy man chased us, asking for money. The driver told us to ignore him, and said we were there at the right time of year, because during the summer the gypsies were out in force to rob you.

The next morning I rented a car. My husband was going to help with the driving, but he "forgot" to bring his driver's license. *How do you forget your driver's license?* It was my first clue that he, too, was nervous about being in Spain.

For a seat of our pants trip, we couldn't have asked for more. Our first parador was in Ronda, and it was an old police station on a cliff, overlooking groves of olives. It was incredible. We could have been happy staying there the entire time. We tried Spanish cuisine, watched a German domino competition—in German—on television, and explored the town with a local guide who used to be a helicopter mechanic. We learned that the only food available in the afternoons were tapas, as most places were closed for siestas. We had a balcony above our room, and we laughed listening to the drunks singing on their way home at night.

My Spanish was nonexistent, so we planned on letting our son speak for us because he had three years of school Spanish. When he finally convinced us that he could hardly read it, let alone speak it, I started listening to CDs three weeks before our trip. I was pretty impressed with myself for being able to order pizza in Madrid the first night. Then my husband discovered tuna fish hidden under the tomato sauce, and asked Colton if his pizza tasted funny. Suddenly it did, and Colt used his Spanish to order from then on. *"No pescado,"* he would say. He also remembered how to say, "extra cheese," or *más queso.*

Exploring Spain was a kick. We stayed long enough in each town to find favorite restaurants and watch soccer on television with the locals. Swimming in the Mediterranean Sea off Nerja was a freezing experience, but Colt and I can say we swam in the Med! I took the elevator back up the cliff to our hotel, and it took forty-five minutes in the shower to get feeling back into my toes and fingers.

The Alhambra was an eye opener for us—we had no idea that the Moors invented air conditioning, solar panels, and irrigation long before modern times. The caves across the valley from the Alhambra were home to over three hundred gypsies, we were told.

The Rock of Gibraltar with its crop of Barbary macaques was equally exciting, as one of the monkeys used my head as a springboard! Underneath Gibraltar, the tunnels reminded me of the

Malinta Tunnel on Corregidor, complete with a hospital and siege tunnels. Now I knew why they called Corregidor the "Gibraltar of the East."

Traveling is full of unknowns, and tensions can run high on vacations. Kevin and I had our arguments and issues on that trip, for sure. I wanted to walk across the runway in Gibraltar—there's even a stoplight to tell you when it's okay to cross. Kevin was afraid of being on an active, international runway. I kept reassuring him, telling him they wouldn't let us cross if it weren't safe, and that there were no planes in the pattern. "What are we going to do if a plane needs to make an emergency landing and we're in the middle of the runway?" he persisted. Exasperated, I turned to him and said, "Run!"

Half an hour later Kevin was on the phone to his sister in Oregon telling her how much fun it was to be on an international runway. *Go figure.*

Kevin had the same unease as we drove through villages on extremely narrow roads, and was unimpressed with my off-route detours for photos of *pueblos blancos* in Andalusia. One night, looking for our parador in Arcos de la Fronterra, we drove around lost for an hour. Colt spotted the parador symbol (⚓) at last, and we wound our way up a one way street to the top of a hill. The parking lot, if that's what you called it, was full. There seemed to be no way down, except a cobblestone path. The desk clerk at our hotel, an old palace, had us park blocking other cars and the roadway, and assured us we would not be towed. Kevin measured our car, and the street we needed to drive down the next morning. There were literally inches between the side of the car and the wall.

As cool as our room in the palace was, the bell tower outside tolled every fifteen minutes. We couldn't imagine trying to sleep if we had to listen to it all night. *What if they towed our car? How would we find it and get it out of impound?* Our nervousness was palpable, but the bell stopped ringing at eleven, our car was still there in the morning, and I drove down the "path" without hitting a wall.

Our next stop was Jerez, home of the Andalusian equestrian ballet. Going to see the dancing horses was memorable, but it was our least favorite part of the trip. I got lost again, turning into a hospital parking lot first, and then an apartment complex. All the signs were in Spanish. When I asked a construction crew for directions, my Spanish CD lessons paid off. I recognized the word *opital* as hospital, and I recognized *derecha* (right) and *izquierda* (left). Back to the hospital, turn right, then left. My husband and son were amazed when I found the horse arena with no more wrong turns, because they hadn't understood a word.

We paid for front row seats and were treated to two hours of prancing, dancing, slobbering, and foaming. It was hard for us to watch how much they used the bit on the horses. Not being horse people, were tired of the show after the first twenty minutes. Now, years later, it is a family joke. Whenever we hear about the dancing horses coming to Portland, Oregon or see them on television, we crack up laughing.

Our son was put off by one waiter's rudeness on our first day driving around. I hadn't realized the olives and bread weren't complimentary. The waiter was impatient and condescending when I asked about them being on the bill. I told Colt that now we knew, and for the rest of the trip we could either accept or decline the olives and bread.

Another day I tried to talk to a local kid on a four-wheeler in Spanish. He ignored me. Then our son said, in English, "I've got a Banshee." The same kid who ignored me said, "You have a Banshee? That is so cool!" He and Colton started talking about four wheelers. I had to laugh.

To me, that's part of traveling. You have to have a thick skin and realize that everything is an adventure. People say that certain cultures are rude, and others are friendly. I think it just depends who you talk to and what kind of mood they're in that day, just like cities and towns in the United States. You stay open minded, and don't take things personally.

Two weeks of exploring Spain flew by, and it was time to go home. Somehow, I found the rental car place in Seville, after recognizing a wall I saw on our carriage ride! Kevin and Colt were astounded. We took a train back to Madrid. Kevin and Colton were ecstatic when they found a McDonalds in the London Gatwick Airport, but they also loved the paella in Nerja. Watching television at home we saw the Ronda's Puente Nuevo bridge on a car commercial, and we all yelled in unison, "We were there! That's our hotel!"

We would go back to Spain in a heartbeat.

Be Spontaneous.

This monkey jumped onto my head.

Tidal waves in the pool.

Antartic Experience-Feb.7th 2008
MS Rotterdam

Yes, the water in Antartica is warm.

TIDAL WAVES

Fifty-foot waves crash around us. Pitching and rolling, our boat is being tossed around like a toy in a bathtub. Half the passengers and crewmembers are sick, and it is like being on a ghost ship, it is so empty. I have no idea why I'm okay, as I've been carsick and seasick over the years. A case of Lladró china tips over and crashes onto the floor outside the gift shop. One of the glass doors in the theater is shattered. Every bar I walked by has liquor and glasses smashed to smithereens. This has to be expensive for Holland America.

I head to the cafeteria, but I stop at the pool deck. Elderly couples are holding on to each other, sloshing through ankle deep water, as lounge chairs slide back and forth on the deck. The Jacuzzis are netted, and giant tidal waves crash end to end in the pool. I'm not as brave as these old folks. I turn around and take the long way to the restaurant, up the stairs and back down on the other side of the pool.

The restaurant is another catastrophe. Stacks of plates are crashing onto the floor, and the waiters are rushing around trying to clean everything up. I find my mother and her friend at a corner table playing cards. I go to sit down with them and a plate of spaghetti comes sliding off a table on the way by. I catch it in midair and become instantly famous as "the girl who caught the spaghetti." I'm fifty-four years old, hardly a girl, but on this cruise, I'm the third youngest person!

I find another friend of my mother's in the bathroom half an hour later and I am shocked to see her tottering around without her cane. I wait for her, and she shoos me out, angry and annoyed, saying she can make it without help—she isn't that old! Five minutes later, I look towards the restroom and see her on the ground. Now I'm angry with myself for obeying her. She's hurt badly, and

I go with her to the infirmary. The ship's doctor wants to airlift her out, but she opts for a few days in bed instead.

I make my way to the front of the ship to watch the waves crash. *Okay, so that was a mistake.* Now I'm feeling queasy. I head for the library, in the middle of the ship, where I find a seat and watch the horizon until I feel better. A library computer crashes to the floor and the screen fractures into a thousand pieces. I remember celebrating my girlfriend Ellen's birthday in Tokyo. A friend gave her a little tomahawk that sounded like glass breaking when you tapped it. A Japanese friend of ours was working the front desk and he borrowed it to tap it on a computer screen. We could hear his coworker scream thinking he broke his computer!

Talking to the crew, I learn that one of the horizontal stabilizers is out and has been for a month. No wonder the ship is so unstable. I can't see how they'll make money with all the damage. In hindsight, was it worth not fixing?

We can't get into the Falkland Islands because of the size of the swells. I really wanted to see the toddler-sized penguins and huge albatrosses in the harbor. There is a silver lining to this cloud. We are now headed to Antarctica where we will spend five days instead of four! Mom and her other friend, Ann, and I are at one of the few tables at the special chef's dinner that evening, and it takes days for the rest of the ship to fully recover.

I HAVE ON my heavy coat, gloves, scarf, and hat. I have two camera batteries in case one dies. Bernard, our biologist on board, is on the public address system telling us about the Gerlache Strait. It's so foggy in Antarctica that we can't see anything. It is like pea soup! Once in a while, a yacht comes out of the soup, but for the most part we see nothingness. There are some research stations, but we turn back because there's not enough visibility for the captain to risk going forward.

The fog begins to lift the next day. I see flying fish everywhere, and take pictures, even though they are far away. Zooming in on my camera screen I see they're not flying fish at all… they're penguins! Penguins are everywhere! Chinstraps, Adélies, and gentoos are swimming and leaping out of the water all around us. There are other birds, too—large albatrosses and Cape petrels with checkered wings.

Seals and whales are lying on icebergs as we motor by. Apparently, some of them eat penguins and some don't. We see some penguins on an iceberg with a seal and Bernard informs us that's a Weddell seal that doesn't eat penguins. I can't tell the difference, but somehow the penguins know. Leopard seals will eat them but Weddells, crabeaters, and Ross seals won't.

We were at Elephant Island last night, and now we are on our way to "Iceberg Alley," arriving at five or six in the morning. *Oh, I hope the sun is out!* The icebergs we saw today had tiny specks on them that turned out to be penguins. Bernard says the dead giveaway for whether there are penguins there or not is to look for pink snow. Penguins eat pink krill, so they poop pink. This is the most exciting trip I've ever been on! I knew a little about Antarctica and Admiral Byrd's trip here in 1926, but not much.

I still hadn't seen an iceberg up close with penguins on it, the one thing I prayed I would get pictures of. Well, today I did. We went right by them! The little gentoos seemed so confused by our huge ship… *Do we run away from it? Do we jump in the water and get eaten by leopard seals, or do we run up the hill we just ran down?* Penguins in nature are nothing like those at the zoo. They still smelled, especially at the large colonies we came upon, but their behavior was much more interesting to watch. The next time I go to Antarctica, I will go on a smaller boat, so that I can get off on the continent and share a hot pool with the penguins.

There is an Antarctic swim in the aft pool today. I expect it to be deserted, but the pool is full of people. Jumping into the warm water I feel like I am in the movie, *Cocoon*. Holland America knows how to pamper its passengers, and the crewmembers are waiting with robes and hot chocolate when we get out. I stay in a long time, swimming with Emily, a teacher who is the second youngest passenger on this ship, and she is thirty years old!

For the last two weeks people have been telling me I'm not the only Northwest pilot on the ship. But people are always getting airlines confused, so I doubt he is with Northwest. I finally give my name and room number to a couple going to the late dinner with him, even though they can't remember his name. The next day there is a note under my door saying to meet him and his wife at a certain bar the next evening.

We have thousands of pilots, so even if he is at Northwest, I don't expect to recognize him, but it will be fun to say hello. Walking into the bar, Doug and his wife Roseanne are waiting for me, and I recognize him! We aren't sure why we know each other, but think we must have flown together. Later I look him up in my logbook at home. We've flown together three or four times, and even had an engine failure on one of our flights and had to land in Taipei. "That was you?" he asks, when I tell him. "Yes, and I remember running into you while I was looking for the pool behind the hotel!" I answer. The good news is that he remembered me as a crewmember, not a woman pilot! The bad news is that we must both be boring people, because we didn't remember each other at all.

Returning to South America, we stop at Cape Horn, one of the most dangerous places on earth. It is dead calm, and the ship circles a few times. We can even feel our own wake as we cross back over it. Bernard tells us it is the bump between the two oceans, caused by the difference in temperature and salinity. We still don't know, to this day, whether he was kidding or not. I am standing on Doug and Roseanne's balcony with them, laughing about the fifty-foot waves we survived, only to be smooth at the Cape.

We love Chilé, and pull into Valparaiso at the end of our trip. A few nights later I am at La Boca in Buenos Aires, ready to fly home the next morning. South America was amazing.

Farewell to thee, Argentina!

EXPECTATIONS

I used to get so excited about going on vacation. Waiting breathlessly, counting down the days, I had every detail of the trip planned. I loved thinking about it ahead of time, and I had each activity and day laid out. I didn't even need to go, because I had already been there over and over for months.

Then the time came. *The real vacation.* It was always a letdown. There was no way it could ever be as good as I hoped. Flights got cancelled or we missed them because we were standby. Tempers were short and the kids were whiny. The activities I thought would be the most fun weren't, and the ones I did on the spur of the moment—just going with the flow—were the best.

Swimming with the dolphins on a Disney cruise is the only planned adventure that exceeded my expectations. Growing up a fan of *Flipper*, the famous dolphin television show, it was a lifelong dream to be able to swim with them. It was incredible being in the water with two, huge dolphins, touching and playing with them. I left the water on cloud nine, sure if this were the last day of my life, I would be fine.

I couldn't wait to show the kids my favorite layover spots in San Francisco. I knew my daughter would love the jazz hangout I found because she was a saxophone player. She would love the painters I loved to watch, creating masterpieces with cans of spray paint and torn cardboard in an alley near Ghirardelli Square. My son would love Alcatraz!

They weren't impressed. Instead, they had their own favorites. What topped their list was... The Bushman! The Bushman is a homeless man who hides behind a branch and jumps out at passersby. I agreed, he was fun to watch, but I never would have guessed he could surpass what I had planned. Standing there, watching them enjoy the moment, I realized I needed to be more present.

Instead of anticipating how much fun it would be to share an experience with my family, I needed to enjoy it for me.

Maybe that's why our best family vacations were the ones to new places where none of us had ever been. Going to Spain, my expectations were initially overshadowed by my immediate concerns: finding the hotels in a country where I didn't speak or read the language. Then I arrived, and it was so memorable and spontaneous that it could never compare with my hopes and dreams. Other than having hotel rooms reserved, nothing was planned. I didn't know about the Alhambra, the Moors, the runway at Gibraltar, or the hundreds of monkeys that live there. You can see Africa from the rock, and they speak English there, not Spanish. Seventy thousand ships pass by each year, so the English won't give it back to Spain. We went on a whim, because we were nearby.

Speaking of languages, I took classes in Japanese so that I could do my PAs on the airplane for our customers. I bought Rosetta Stone for Italy, tapes and CDs for Korea, and I had years of French in school. There was no way I could learn all the languages for every country I flew to over the years. Learning Chinese or Japanese should have been a priority for me ahead of Spanish, but I was glad I was "forced" into it. I always learned the basics before I went to a new country: Hello, thank you, you're welcome, excuse me, and goodbye. Most of the hotels in Asia had a "cheat" card and the front desk personnel always helped with pronunciation. The cheat card also had the hotel's name on it, so I could hand it to any cab driver if I needed to get back to my room.

Travel is fun because it is so unpredictable. My husband would disagree. Driving a rental car in a strange place like Scotland, Spain, Italy, or New Zealand, I had no choice but to be 'present,' especially when driving on the 'wrong' side of the road. And I do mean unpredictable, not dangerous. Dangerous is not fun for me. Some friends of mine went to Syria, Jordan, and Egypt for vacation. They said, "Never again will we go on a vacation where we have to worry about dying. At least five times I thought it was the end—that we were going to be shot and killed."

My daughter likes living 'on the edge', but I don't. An adrenaline rush is not a vacation to me. I get plenty of adrenaline from harried flights or unforecasted weather conditions while piloting an airplane. To me, vacations are about seeing new things and having unforgettable experiences. Sometimes they are just to relax and unwind. But they are never meant to be close encounters with death.

I want to go on a photo safari in Africa. I have my preconceived notions of the trip, of course. I want close encounters with animals and new experiences. My idea of a safari is a safe, five-star, controlled adventure. I do not want to get sick or charged by a rhino. I'll read some background history to help understand what I see, without dissecting or planning what will happen each day. I'll learn enough to pack what I need, and I will plan lenses and photo equipment. But that's it. I won't overthink it, so I won't be disappointed.

Planning is overrated.

I didn't even know what gannets were until we saw them in New Zealand.

I never liked penguins in zoos, but in the wild they are amazing!

SYNCHRONICITY

The best part about traveling, once I overcome preconceived notions and expectations, is the synchronicity. I can't get over how well things work once I let go of control. Our cruise from Auckland, New Zealand through Tahiti and the Cook Islands is a prime example. Starting with the cab ride to the dock, our three-week cruise across the Pacific until we docked in Long Beach, California was a lesson in synchronicity.

Everything on the Regency cruise was paid for… the flight over, the tips, the shore excursions, the food in any dining area of the ship, the booze… everything except our internet charges and $999 upgrade to first class. The ship was beautiful. We had a balcony room with a walk-in closet.

The welcome reception the first night was top notch with lobster, crab, and shrimp hors d'oeuvres. One of the waiters looked familiar, like a friend of mine named Noel from the Antarctica cruise. I read his nametag. *It was him!*

His recognition was instantaneous. "Kathy! Where is your mom? Is she with you? How are you?" I couldn't believe he remembered me.

Our first stop was the Bay of Islands in New Zealand. Kevin and I just walked around the island with no idea where we were going as I snapped pictures. We walked down a hill to a beach, and I found a red rubber ball floating on the waves. No one was around, so I snagged it and bounced it all the way back to the ship's tender, much to my husband's embarrassment.

"You aren't taking that ball on the ship," he announced.

"I might. I'll give it some kid."

"Just how many kids have you seen on our ship?"

"We just boarded last night. None so far." *I hate it when he's right.*

As luck would have it, we had just missed a tender and it would be a half hour until the next one. We headed for the ice cream shop by the pier. Standing in line, a little boy in a stroller looked up at me and said, in awe, "Ball. Soccer ball."

I asked his dad if he could have it.

"Are you kidding? We've been driving around for two weeks in a camper van and that's all he has been asking for... a red soccer ball. Do you think we could find a toy store that has one? You're a life saver!"

I gave the ball to the little boy, but not before giving my husband the "See, I told you so" look.

The next day was spent at sea and we decided to go for a swim. The movement of the ship created a huge wave in the pool, and it looked fun. There was a lady swimming already, with a snorkel and mask. It was pretty rough to be practicing, I thought. I jumped in and talked to her. Her name was Susan and she had lost the diamond in her wedding ring and was looking for it. She was ready to give up. It was just too rough.

I told her I would look for it if she leant me her mask. The doubt was written on her face, but she handed me the mask and told me her room number so I could bring it back to her. "You better take your rings off, though," she said. "The motion of water will knock your stones out, too." *I should have listened to her.*

The pool was small and was easy to swim around, even with the waves. I swam close to the bottom, searching. The waves kept moving me, but I caught a sparkle out of the corner of my eye. I slammed my hand down onto the bottom of the pool just as the ship rolled with the wave. Closing my fingers around it, I headed for the surface. Carefully I opened my hand. It was the diamond!

Susan was commiserating with another couple on the deck. Her husband was angry with her, she was saying. I climbed out of the pool and told her not to give up yet. Then I placed my hand on top of hers and dropped the diamond into it

She started screaming for joy, scaring everyone on the pool deck! Then she started hugging and thanking me over and over. It was a $7000 diamond, a surprise present from her husband with a huge story behind it, she said. They had just replaced her old ring and had not insured this one yet. She was beside herself, and took off to find her husband.

I jumped back in the water with a huge smile on my face. It is so cool to make someone that happy! I swam back to the same spot, near the drain, without the mask, and felt around on the bottom. It seemed like a little swirl or current in that area, as there was dirt and a piece of rubber, too. This time I found a gold earring. I took it to the bartender to put in the lost and found.

On the way back to the pool, a lady in the Jacuzzi asked me what was wrong with the screaming lady. I told her, and she said she had just lost a $400 gold earring from her favorite pair. I retrieved the earring from the bartender for her. *What a crazy day.*

I jumped back in the water, only to realize that my amethyst was missing from one of my rings. Great, just great. I knew where to look… the sweet spot… but it wasn't there. I could find everyone else's treasures except my own. Dejected, I kept swimming around until my fingers were pruning. It was time to get out. I took one more shot at the sweet spot… and found my amethyst!

The word of what happened spread like wildfire on the ship. Just like the Antarctica cruise, I was famous, but not for being a female pilot or saving a plate of spaghetti or taking great penguin pictures. The oddest, and saddest, part of the whole experience was the number of people who came up to me afterwards and asked why I hadn't kept the diamond. "She never would have known," they said.

"I would have known," I answered.

First Noel, then the red rubber ball, and then the diamond and earring. I was floating on air. I love synchronicity, even though some call it luck or coincidence. The rest of the cruise was the same. I had extra tickets for excursions—somehow we had doubles of everything. I turned them in at the desk, and the lady behind the counter was thrilled. She had unhappy people who wanted those exact tickets. She knew that I had let another couple go in our place the day before because the excursions were sold out, and thanked me profusely. I told her yesterday had worked out better by giving the tickets away. I had an incredible dolphin adventure instead, and I was the only patron. I fed the retired Navy dolphins their vitamins, checked their vitals, and learned so much. Someone had told her about the diamond. "Are you an angel?" she asked. *I wish.*

Everyone on the snorkeling boat knew about the diamond, because Susan and the earring lady were both there, pointing me out Snorkeling in Tahiti was amazing. One man was so excited to be swimming with sting rays that he could hardly contain himself. I took lots of pictures of him, just because he was so entertaining. Then, later, I couldn't find him to give them to him.

On the last day of the cruise I spotted him. I chased him down, and told him I had pictures of him on the snorkeling trip. He hadn't gone snorkeling, he said, and then vented his anger and frustration to me. Someone had stolen his camera and he didn't have any pictures of the cruise. I showed him the pictures of the man with the stingrays. "Wait a minute, I did go swimming with the stingrays! Just not snorkeling." He was so excited that I had pictures, because that was the best part of his trip! I couldn't find his camera, but I did give him copies of all the pictures he wanted of places we had been on the cruise. It was unforgettable.

Synchronicity. Go figure.

Noel and me

EXPLOSIONS

I was the copilot on a Northwest Airlines flight into the Tampa International Airport on January 28, 1986. The Challenger was lifting off as we neared our destination. It was so exciting to be in the air at the same time as the space shuttle. We could see it from the cockpit! The captain had me make the announcements to the 146 people in the back of our full Boeing 727. I keyed the microphone and relayed everything ATC said. We were glued to the scene outside our window, and felt the plane lean left as 146 people crowded that side to look, too.

When the Challenger exploded seventy-three seconds after takeoff, we thought it had just gone out of sight. Then ATC informed us that it had blown up with no known survivors. All seven crewmembers were dead.

Growing up, I had felt such pride in our space program. There were cards and trinkets in our cereal boxes, and we always watched the liftoffs on television at school or at home. The Challenger mission was a widely publicized launch. After all, Christa McAuliffe was on board—the first teacher to go up in space. Millions of people were watching the launch across the nation, including thousands of school children. I didn't want to tell the passengers what had happened, but I had to.

My voice cracked as I relayed the news. When we landed in Tampa, there wasn't a dry eye on the plane. As the people deplaned and stepped onto the jet bridge, they were all crying or in shock. It was horrible.

The day went down in my book as unforgettable. I met my childhood friend, Sally, for a subdued lunch at the airport before returning to Minneapolis. We cried. When it was later determined that a faulty O ring seal was the cause of the accident, I cried again. *An O ring!*

FLYING OVER THE ocean between Taiwan and Mainland China in 1995 and 1996 during the Taiwan Strait Crisis brought back the Challenger explosion memories for me. What if we were hit by a missile? The area was always active, and sometimes we were vectored around, but usually not. What would the news have to say? Many pilots believed the TWA 800 incident was a missile and not an explosion caused by the scavenge pumps sparking in the center fuel tank. I had seen the center tank low-pressure lights blinking for years without an explosion, so I didn't believe it either. Scud missiles were fired at planes delivering troops and supplies during the Gulf War, and I decided not to fly the military routes at our company. A 747 is a huge target for a missile, and I had young children at home. Would the truth be told if we were hit in the Straits of Taiwan?

WE PRACTICE A lot of denial as pilots, and 9/11 is proof of that. We never considered the possibility that our planes could be used as bombs.

Denial is not a river in Egypt.

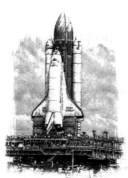

SAFETY

I always wanted to see more of the Philippines, but with the kidnappings and horror stories reported in the media, I never did. I'm a chicken. I stay with a group when I go out at night, or I don't leave the hotel. I know women pilots who have been raped in Seoul and beaten up in Munich. Women are too easily victimized, and I don't like feeling afraid. I will stay in my hotel room alone rather than take an unnecessary risk.

Captains have told me how inexpensive the resorts are in Jamaica, but a vacation surrounded by razor-wire fences with armed guards patrolling them isn't worth the money I would save. I think back to my experiences in Batam, Indonesia after 9/11. Being fearful isn't a relaxing vacation.

I like safe vacations. Zip-lining in Costa Rica was a stretch for me until I saw how safe and well-designed the system was. The zip-lines were doubled, covered with rubber, and secured strongly around giant trees. There were well built platforms and railings. It was a blast!

Despite my layers of precautions, I was robbed in broad daylight in 2008. The scary part was the aggressiveness of the gypsy woman who pickpocketed me in Bologna, Italy. She had me backed against a wall in an isolated tourist spot by the tower. And it wasn't that I wasn't prepared or was fooled by her—she had a five-month-old baby in her arms that I didn't want to hurt fending her off! I knew better than to be there alone, yet there I was. I called out to a couple of American students who saved me, but still… I thought I was dressed down, and unobtrusive, but my camera gave me away. My money and credit cards were in my bra purse, and the rest of my cash was in a zipper pocket in my socks, so I only lost fifty euros, about thirty-five dollars U.S.

We can all get into a jam no matter how careful we are.

I liked it when Singaporeans assumed I was Australian. Now I check the U.S. State Department Overseas Advisory Council website for updates and current hot spots. They are always changing. Mexico is on the list, but only certain areas in Mexico. I use AAA for information, too, and you don't have to be a member to purchase safety items in their stores and check out the latest advisories.

Once, on a layover in Bangkok, our flight crew took the Chao Phraya River tour. A family waved to us, smiling as we went by. When I turned around to take their picture, they were flipping us off… giving us the bird! As they say in Thailand, there are many ways to smile.

The guys I flew with joked that I had a girlfriend in every city. I did, and I think being with a local helped me stay safe. One month I had Boston layovers and I always met my Aunt Jane, who lived in Cambridge. On the last weekend of the month, my aunt decided to meet me at the hotel. The captain went inside first, while I waited for my bags. When I got to the lobby I found him putting the move on my Aunt Jane! "So, who are you waiting for, pretty lady? Need some company?" he asked her.

"Well, I'm waiting for her," she said, pointing at me. Boy, did his face turn red when she told him she was my Aunt Jane. I didn't realize the other pilots thought I was having an affair and that "Aunt Jane" was their "wink and smile" name for girlfriend.

One of my best girlfriends, Akiko, lives near the hotel in Narita, Japan. Akiko and her family have even been to visit us in Oregon three times. I met her one night while she was waiting tables in her restaurant down the street. The men assumed she didn't speak English, and were quite rude, calling "Sapporo, Mamisan," with no *kudasai* (please) or *domo arrigato* (thank you). I felt sorry for her. Eventually, we were the only table left as the restaurant emptied out. Akiko came over and asked in perfect English, "So, are you really a pilot?" Akiko was educated in Cambridge, England and spoke excellent English. We started having coffee every morning we could, and some days she drove me places I never would have seen on my own. Other days we just ran errands, but that was fun, too. When I had more time we would hike up a mountain, tour a temple, go to the "Street of Dreams" designer homes, or visit her mom and sister in Chiba City.

We've had pilots—tough guys—shot, kidnapped, and robbed on layovers. I don't kid myself. Of course it could happen to me.

I met a woman who was a marketing director for her company. The company was sending her to an isolated factory in the Philippines and thought that she should have a man on her team, for safety. She was furious—incensed that they thought she needed a man. She insisted on going to the work site with only the three women she was with. I never saw her on another flight, and I hope she was okay. I'm liberated, but not stupid. There are places in this world that are dangerous for women or men to go alone.

A female airline pilot in Dubai was speaking on her phone. The cab driver heard her say the "F" word, and drove her to the police station where she was arrested and booked. *Yes, booked. She lost her job.*

A flight attendant in our language class complained about the reaction of Japanese men to her jogging in short, silky shorts. They made lewd comments and gestures, even masturbating, as she ran by. She wanted to know how to say, "Get lost, asshole!" in Japanese. Our language instructor suggested she wear a little more when she jogs as, after all, it is their culture in their country. The flight attendant was furious. Why should she have to change her habits when she wasn't doing anything wrong? I would have handled the situation differently. I respect other people's customs, especially in their country. Besides, there is no reason to ask for trouble. Be careful, not foolish. Pay for the workout rooms and the swimming pool if need be. Or exercise on the hotel grounds or in your room. You can't put a price on your life.

Be smart. Be safe. Be careful.

Spend your money on comfortable hotel rooms.

Don't take a room on the first floor.

Tell the front desk not to give anyone your room key or information.

Search the room before bolting the door, with a friend waiting in the hall.

Get an inexpensive ratchet-lock for your hotel door.

Don't advertise your home country on your suitcase.

Get a business card at the front desk.

Don't carry a purse—use your tight, front pockets.

Don't dress like an American.

Have the hotel call a safe, reputable taxi.

Put a whistle on your key chain or in your pocket.

Don't act like a target. Walk confidently.

Never drop your guard, but stay open to opportunity.

Have fun!

ISIS + ISA+21

Twenty-one lady airline pilots met in Las Vegas, Nevada in 1978. They came up with their very creative name: ISA+21. How things have changed. Everyone used to know what ISA+21 meant, and now they all look at you like you have just said ISIS. The acronym ISA means International Standard Atmosphere, and the +21 means twenty-one degrees above standard.

I was hired by a major airline in 1981 and was invited to join, but I was in a bad marriage with no extra cash. And I didn't want to be part of a group of women airline pilots when I was trying so hard to fit in with the guys. But those weren't my only reasons. Later, when I had the money, my kids had birthdays that fell on the conference dates. If I couldn't go to the conferences, I couldn't meet anyone in the group. *Why pay dues for something I couldn't go to?*

When I finally joined in 2011, I realized how foolish I had been. What could be more fun than traveling with a group of girlfriends who have the same career as you? Especially if your spouse can't go with you because it is his busy time of year and he is working?

I have traveled overseas with this group to Amsterdam, Austria, Czech Republic, Germany, Hungary, and Italy. On this continent we have met in Arizona, British Columbia, California, Colorado, New Jersey, New York, Ontario, Texas, Washington, and Washington DC.

I've learned a lot in an all-women's group. I've learned that we need to support each other more and criticize each other less. I've learned we are all so different that it makes my head spin. ISA+21 has lost members along the way because of personality clashes, but what group will you ever be a part of where everyone gets along? Mostly I've made new friends and had an amazing time. I enjoy this group so much that I am now on their board of directors.

Becoming an airline pilot is such an expensive and difficult journey that many women, especially single mothers, need help paying for their ratings. ISA+21 members have donated over a million dollars to women who want to be airline pilots. It's great to be able to make a difference.

Traveling with this group I never know what I am going to learn, do, or see. My favorite activity was Segwaying in Dresden. That opened me up to off-road Segwaying in Hawaii on the North Shore with my husband.

I loved Pompeii and the Blue Grotto in Italy. I didn't want to see the Leaning Tower of Pisa because it is such a touristy place. Luckily my girlfriend convinced me to go while we were staying at a farmhouse in Tuscany. It's not just a leaning tower tourist trap, it's a bell tower in a square of miracles.

Going to Texas with my husband to visit our nephew and his family, I knew about Fredericksburg because our group had gone, and I knew the guys would love the National Museum of the Pacific War.

I used to live in California, but I had never been to Santa Barbara, and seeing the missions brought back memories of my favorite book when I was a teen, Island of the Blue Dolphins.

Being with a group where everything is all planned out is easy, and I learn more when I am on tours and there is a guide. After a board meeting in Amsterdam, I wasn't ready to go home, so I booked a Viator tour of Ireland. The weather was incredible, with no rain, and I saw the peninsulas in full sunshine!

I didn't want to go home after Berlin and Dresden either, so four of us took a train to Munich. My nephew and his wife met me for a late lunch by the Rathaus-Glockenspiel. They couldn't stay, but I had booked a guided photo tour of Munich for the evening. When you book a private tour on the Internet, you never know what you are getting, or how safe it is. I left the information and the guy's picture at home on my desk just in case I disappeared. I was thrilled when one of my girlfriends ended up being able to go along. It was incredible. The man's name was Dave, and he taught me more in three hours than I had learned all year using my new Nikon.

The next three days I had booked a trip along the Romantic Road, stopping at Neuschwanstein, the castle Walt Disney modeled his after. My hotel room in Hohenschwangau looked out at the castle at night. I couldn't find anyone to go with me, but sometimes that's better with the number of photos I take. I loved the town of Rothenburg, and went on the night watchman tour. One thousand photos later, I headed home.

Two weeks after my trip, my husband's cousin called and asked me how my photo tour was with Dave. "How did you know about that?" I asked him.

"Well, you know that friend of mine you met in the airport last year, Alex?" He's Dave's best man at his wedding and I'm watering his garden while he's gone."

"Wait, that can't be the same guy. Dave is already married," I said.

"That was his American wedding. This is his German one."

Unbelievable.

But how did Dave and Alex get on the subject of me? I emailed Dave. "He asked me if I had done anything fun lately, and I told him yes. I gave a photo tour to two lady airline captains. He wanted to know if one of them was Kathy McCullough!"

Seriously? Not only is it a small world, but it's a crazy fun one!

Synchronicity, again.

Swimming with turtles and dolphins.

BUCKET LIST, SCHMUCKET LIST

I've never had a bucket list. I still don't. A bucket list would limit my experiences. How do you know you want to do something if you've never heard about it? Why would you want to do something if you're too afraid and overthink it?

Swimming with sharks was something I would never do on purpose. Doing aerobatics in a glider was something I never considered either because I get sick after a few maneuvers. Being on a *Deadliest Catch* crab boat was a big no. Flying as captain on a 747 wasn't on my bucket list, either, but I've done all these things and more.

I never thought about taking a helicopter ride into the Grand Canyon. I'd heard too many stories about wind gusts and low time pilots crashing into canyon walls. Then a girlfriend of mine, a pilot I trusted, moved to Las Vegas to fly helicopter tours. Going into the Grand Canyon with Emily at the helm was incredible, indescribably beautiful, and safe.

I always wanted to swim with Flipper, but I never dreamed I could swim with dolphins because I didn't know you could. Then I got a Christmas card with a picture of my girlfriend's daughter swimming with dolphins in the Bahamas. I called and made arrangements for a dolphin swim because our next cruise was going to the Bahamas! It was the most money I'd ever spent on an activity, but so worth it.

I didn't have time to back out because it was impulsive. When I overthink things, I don't do them. I thought I was swimming with sting rays, not sharks, until it was time to jump in and the sharks were there, too. Everyone else was doing it and they were just nurse sharks.

The aerobatic glider instructor had a solution for my weak stomach... we would take turns! As long as I'm flying I don't get sick. And who knew there was an old crab boat that was being used on shore excursions in Alaska? We had so much fun crabbing, feeding eagles, and catching fish on an Indian reservation where it was legal!

There are things I would love to do some day, but I won't call it a bucket list:

Go on a five-star African safari
Photograph ruins in Cambodia and Mexico
Go to Niagara Falls when it is frozen
Jet boat on the Snake River
Swim with manatees
Stay in a hut on a tropical pier in Fiji
Go to Santorini, Greece

Part of the reason I don't believe in a bucket list is that I wouldn't know where to start. I just wake up and go for it! My bucket list is much more intangible:

Keep learning and growing.
Keep loving people, animals and life.
Keep embracing other cultures.
Keep traveling everywhere.
Keep living life to the fullest.

My motto is:

Never say never.

REVERSE BUCKET LIST

I've changed so much in my life that a bucket list would have been worthless. You couldn't have convinced my young self that having children would be the best part of my life. *But it was.* And being a mom kept me 'senior' enough to fly some of the best trips on the airline—long layovers in Singapore, Hong Kong, Saipan, and Seoul so that I could be home for weeks at a time instead of days. I swore I would never commute, yet I am still living in the middle of nowhere, and loving it.

I was never a goal setter. That may seem odd for someone who became an airline pilot, but it is true.

I learned to fly for fun, because I wanted to fly my girlfriends to the beach for lunch. There was a runway across the street from Venice Beach where I loved to hunt shark's teeth, and that was the other reason. I kept flying for the same reason: *fun.* A few years later I had so much flying time and so many ratings that everyone kept telling me to get an airline job. I didn't think I could because I wore glasses and my eyes were 20/30. The airlines required pilots to have 20/20 vision.

Northwest Airlines hired me in 1981, when they dropped their eye requirement to 20/70. For twenty-five years I traveled the world and got paid to do it. I'm proud to say I "hit the ground running" on almost every layover of my career. Looking back, I can't believe the places my life has taken me. The end result is a reverse bucket list bigger than my wildest dreams.

Looking at a picture of Siam from my favorite travel book as a child, there is a boat, a temple, and a child riding an elephant. When I did all these things in Thailand, it was a dream come true. Isn't that what a bucket list really is? Bringing your dreams to life? Dreams you've forgotten you had?

What follows is a list of some of the best things I've ever done. These things would have been on my bucket list if I had only known how fun they were before I did them. This is my *completed bucket list:*

Ride an elephant in Thailand

Explore Tahiti's beaches and mountains

See the Singapore Zoo, day and night

Take a photo class in Venice, Italy

Stay in Camogli, Italy on the Italian Riviera

Walk to the earth pyramids in Oberbozen, Italy on a snowy morn

Hike all around Kaikoura Peninsula, NZ before the earthquake

Watch the gannets feed their new babies at Piha Beach, NZ

Feed petrels, eagles, and giant albatrosses

Dig my own hot pool on the Coromandel Peninsula, NZ

Find magnetic black sand on the beach at Piha

Snorkel in Florida's crystal-clear springs and see 100 feet down

Jump waves for hours all over the world

Collect thousands of shells in Sanibel Island, Florida

Tube the Ichetucknee River

(as a moccasin swims between my little brother's legs)

Strain shark's teeth from the surf at Venice Beach

after flying there in my Cessna 140

Watch Niagara Falls, Canada out of my hotel room window

Take a cooking class in Singapore

Venture into the tunnels of Korea, the Philippines,

and Crescent Beach (with rattlesnakes)

Cruise the Caribbean

Walk around Goblin Valley, Utah

Explore Arches National Park

Fly into the Grand Canyon in a helicopter and land

Observe a Magellanic penguin colony from a boardwalk in Chile

Swim with sea turtles in Hawaii

See the Grand Canyon and Bryce Canyon in the snow

Watch gentoo penguins dive off icebergs

Walk through a grove of rainbow gum trees on Maui

Fly over the Big Island volcano in a helicopter
Take off over the South China Sea at sunrise
See monkeys in the trees in Indonesia
Watch wild cockatoos fly in Singapore
Pet a llama in South America
Be backstage at rock concerts
Ski on mountains in Colorado, New Mexico, and Oregon
Fly Jack Mould home in a Beaver floatplane
Land on a glacier in Alaska
Hike the Olympics and Vancouver Island
Walk on railroad tracks to a hidden waterfall
See the Alhambra in Granada, Spain
Stay on a cliff top parador in Ronda
Relax in a pool with a swim-up bar and underwater music
Swim all over the world, including the Mediterranean Sea
Waterslide backwards at the Pacific Island Club in Saipan
Ride a horse in the Puerto Rican rainforest
Stay on an island in northern Ontario, Canada
Hike around Lake Louise, Canada
Snorkel the South Pacific, Hawaii, Florida Keys, and the Marianas
Swim with sharks and sting rays in Tahiti
Four-wheel in Tahiti, New Zealand, and Oregon
Waterski on a deserted river of glass and in a canyon
Whitewater raft in Oregon and Washington
Hold wild animals at a park in Bandon
Stay on Crater Lake
Jet boat on the Rogue River, doing spins
Collect cuttlefish and soccer balls in England
Explore castles in Europe and Asia
Segway in Hawaii and Germany
Walk the canals of the Netherlands
See the clocks from "Longitude" at the Tower Bridge
Boat through glowworm caves in New Zealand
Watch grizzlies eat sedge grass in Alaska
Boat the Alaskan fjords to see otters and whales

Dance the tango in Buenos Aires
Watch Fourth of July fireworks at the Lincoln Memorial
Spend New Year's Eve in Times Square—never again!
Swim with the dolphins
Watch humpbacks, orcas, and gray whales
Raft with turtles and dolphins
Drink Limoncella in Italy
Ride limousines in Singapore
Watch the Portage Glacier "calve"
Drive in Scotland, Spain, Italy, and New Zealand
Go through the Panama Canal
Hold a sloth
See a wild porcupine at the dunes
And so much more!

THIS IS THE tip of the proverbial iceberg of my life. My reverse bucket list is made up of memories. I can always add to it, but then the book would go on forever with some mundane and ordinary moments that were stellar to me. I remember:

A neighborhood Halloween party in our basement before Dad died
Fishing for bluegill in Indiana at my grandparent's house
Catching fireflies
Playing croquet (and sledding!)
on my grandparent's hill with the river below
Reading in a live oak tree over a pond in Florida
Playing Legos with my kids
Having picnics down in the canyon near a ghost house
Lying on the trampoline watching a meteor shower
Sitting in the Jacuzzi listening to coyotes howl
Living in the middle of nowhere
Having children
Raising a litter of puppies

Bottle feeding a calf, a baby jack rabbit, and kittens
Finding great horned owls

HONESTLY, IF I died today there is no way I could complain about my life and its wonders and joys. Just writing this, my heart soars and I feel blessed and happy.

Find your joy. Make your life the best it can be. Don't dwell on what could have been or what should be. Wake up thankful and happy for what you have.

Put memories in your bucket instead of dreams!

Our hotel in Ronda, Spain

Lantau Island, Hong Kong, China

HOME SWEET HOME

There's no place like home; there's no place like home. I'm sure my husband is ready for home after a week or so, while I am happy to stay a month or two. No matter how much fun I have on vacation, there is no place like home. I sleep the best sleep I've had in days, or weeks, and truly relax.

When the hotel room beds are too small, too hard, or just plain uncomfortable, I would rather be home. But when I'm on a beach in Hawaii, that's home to me. (Unless the elephants above us are stampeding and impeding my sleep. Did you know that Hawaii doesn't have the access to concrete to build that you would expect? That most of the condos are made of wood, and the downstairs units are noisier?)

Who complains about vacations? I'm not complaining. I'm not even venting. I'm just saying, it's a good sign that you're glad to be home. It means you're happy where you are and love the home you've created. I love to travel because I learn so much, see so many people I love, and do new things. I come home with new thoughts, new ideas, and good memories.

I get home and do the bare minimum the first night. I snuggle with my dog, who has not suffered at all staying at our son's house. I stretch out and enjoy the peace and quiet. I take deep breaths and truly relax. There's no reason to stress about the mess. The loads of wash and the chaos of unpacking can wait.

My mom used to clean the refrigerator and make the beds with clean sheets before a vacation. She said she enjoyed the vacation more, although leaving was stressful with Dad honking the horn to hurry her along!

The next morning, I start a load of laundry, file the receipts, and put the toiletries in the bathroom. I take the little soaps and shampoos to the mudroom to give away, and I put away the presents I've gotten for friends on vacation. Room by room I tackle the clutter and chaos, with a cup of coffee and good music in the background.

Visions of my vacation fill my head as I restore order in my house. Whether it is elephants or penguins, ski slopes or tropical beaches, there's no place like home. But there is also nothing like traveling. This world is an incredible place to explore.

There's no place like home.

Made in the USA
San Bernardino, CA
14 March 2018